Like Streams to the Ocean

Like Streams to the Ocean

NOTES ON EGO, LOVE, AND THE THINGS THAT MAKE US WHO WE ARE

≈≈≈

JEDIDIAH JENKINS

CONVERGENT

NEW YORK

Published in the United States by Convergent Books,
an imprint of Random House, a division of
Penguin Random House LLC, New York.

CONVERGENT BOOKS is a registered trademark and
its C colophon is a trademark of Penguin Random House LLC.

LIBRARY OF CONGRESS CATALOGING-IN-PUBLICATION DATA
Names: Jenkins, Jedidiah, author.
Title: Like streams to the ocean: notes on ego, love, and the things
that make us who we are / Jedidiah Jenkins.
Description: New York: Convergent, [2020]
Identifiers: LCCN 2020012014 (print) | LCCN 2020012015 (ebook) |
ISBN 9780593137239 (hardcover) | ISBN 9780593137246 (ebook)
Subjects: LCSH: Jenkins, Jedidiah. | Introspection. | Self. |
Self (Philosophy) | Conduct of life.
Classification: LCC BF316 .J46 2020 (print) | LCC BF316 (ebook) |
DDC 814/.6—dc23
LC record available at https://lccn.loc.gov/2020012014
LC ebook record available at https://lccn.loc.gov/2020012015

Illustrations by Jedidiah Jenkins

Printed in the United States of America on acid-free paper

convergentbooks.com

2 4 6 8 9 7 5 3 1

First Edition

*For my brother, Luke, who's so good that
all my evil never tainted his good.*

*For those friends who light up my group texts,
who keep me laughing alone and reading articles and
sharpening my mind and cursing at autocorrect for
ruining a joke. Who rally to hold a broken heart.*

Contents

Introduction

Sometimes I wish I could stop thinking and exist in the full contentment of an animal. I envy the staring of a lizard, how it sits in the sun and looks out onto the world. It is not worried about things it can imagine. It is not smiling. It is not happy at its contentment. How could it be? It doesn't know discontent. If it is scared, it is scared for a reason, for a danger it can sense and see. It is not imagining what could happen ten years from now. Its mind is perfectly present. Free.

But we are not like that. We are conscious. We are self-aware. We have a triad of worlds inside us: our mind in the present, our mind holding the past, and our mind guessing at the future. Our consciousness unites these things in a mysterious and muddled way. It feels things it cannot explain—urges and sadness and lusts without names. We have to sort out these many longings and instincts, or live in anxious confusion.

For a sentient unicorn such as you or me, the unexamined life is a curse. It leaves the mind at the mercy of the gut, cluttered with confusing information coming from below.

Who we are cannot be fully realized until we tidy up the room and see what's under all those piles of clothes.

The summer before my first book came out, I got very sick. I had a 105-degree fever. At night, I soaked the bed with so much sweat that I started sleeping on six towels, peeling them away when they became unbearably soggy. Over two months of this, I lost twenty-five pounds. I went to the hospital ten times and had enough blood drawn to deflate a whale. They couldn't figure out what was wrong with me.

The illness came at the worst possible time, in the ramp-up to the release of my memoir. In the book, I had written about my struggle to be a good church kid from Tennessee in a family who loved me but thought being gay was a death sentence. For weeks, I had been going back and forth with my mother about things she didn't like in the book. Things she thought were unfair representations and caricatures. When she confronted me, it led to an exchange of no-holds-barred emails, in which I spelled out my homosexuality, the dismantling of my faith, and the new boundaries I needed to set with her. Much of it for the first time. She was willing to listen, but wounded, and she wrote with a firmness in what her faith said about me. By the end, I basically told her I was prepared to walk away from the family.

I remember shaking as I typed those emails. I love no one more than I love my mother, which is why she can rock me and warp my spine. I knew I had a story to tell, one that I'd desperately needed to read when I was younger. But the book was about to blow up my relationship with my family, and now my body was falling apart.

My mystery illness reminded me of a universal truth: It is good to have a doctor for a friend. Toby is that doctor for me. I met him in San Francisco through my old roommate and reveled in his stories from the hospital. He's worked in the emergency room for years, and my god, the things he has seen. The things people stuff into their bodies' orifices are impressively varied (ex: a dead crow, because it was "cold"). Toby's experiences in the ER have made him calm and rational at all times.

After my fever had kept me up for two full weeks, I texted Toby. He told me to get my blood tested. Maybe it was Lyme disease. After the third week, he said, "This is odd, most fevers are gone after two weeks." I kept getting more blood tests, stool tests, urine tests. Negative. Nothing. I was as healthy as an athlete, except for the fact that I was too weak to walk to the bathroom. At six weeks, Toby no longer sounded calm and collected. He was worried, tired of my local doctors not taking this seriously. He told me to go to the ER. If I told them I'd been having chest pain—which was true by then—they would fast-track me to see the doctor.

I poured myself into an Uber and hobbled into the ER. The doctor looked at my most recent test results with a furrowed brow. "You could have testicular cancer," he said, looking up from the sheet. "Drop your pants please so I can check."

"Cancer?"

"Yes. The fever could be your body's way of trying to cook it and kill it."

Wow. I had thought I had a flu, maybe, or Lyme disease. Cancer never crossed my mind. I stood up and pulled down my pants and underwear. The doctor felt around while I braced to hear words that would change my life.

"I feel nothing; that's good. But you could still have cancer. Let me order you a CT scan."

I went home buzzing with mortality. I called Toby. He told me that I'd entered into a category called FUO, Fever of Unknown Origin. This is like unlocking a secret level in a videogame. Suddenly, all kinds of bad things are on offer to explain what's wrong with you: extrapulmonary tuberculosis, typhoid fever, malaria, chronic active hepatitis, HIV/ AIDS, leukemia, lymphoma, colon cancer, testicular carcinoma, and more.

After a horrible week of waiting and wondering, the scan came back negative. My body was frying itself, and no one could figure it out. Toby called and checked on me multiple times a day.

Then, eleven weeks into my illness—the week my book came out—the sickness vanished. Poof. Lifted like a fog.

I went back to the doctor to make sure it could really disappear like that. He wasn't fazed. "Believe it or not, this happens all the time," he said. "People get better, and we never find out what happened." I was baffled, annoyed that modern medicine couldn't tell me what was wrong. "We have a robot driving around on the surface of Mars right now, and you can't tell me why I was sick?" I said.

"We know a lot," he said, "and if you remained sick, we would keep testing. But when people get better, they stop getting tested. And it stays a mystery."

Toby agreed with that doctor. In his controlled and toneless way, I could hear how relieved he was.

Later that week, I talked with my friend Connie, who, like most of my friends, had been really worried about me.

She brought up a possibility I hadn't considered. "I bet it was psychological," she said.

"No way," I said. My sickness had been real. Toby wouldn't have checked on me every day if it was some made-up thing. This wasn't mental.

"Think about it," Connie said. "You're about to release a very personal memoir, one that you're afraid might hurt your relationship with your mom and family. You're always saying that you don't feel emotions, but the body knows. They get stored up."

I didn't believe her then, but here I am a year later, and I am convinced she was right. The book was published. My mother didn't disown me. Somehow, it brought our family closer. At the time, however, I didn't know that would happen. So my body took the reins from my mind. It shut me down.

Psychologists believe that between the ages of eight and ten, we wake up into a sense of self. These are the years when our brains develop a distinct identity. We realize that we aren't our mothers. That we are individuals with one life that ends in death. This is a frightening experience. As individuals, it is our job to stay alive. Mom won't be there forever. So, we observe the world around us for danger. It is that world, the one we map in those opening years, that we spend the rest of our lives trying to fix. I didn't know this when I got sick, but when I heard it later, it clicked.

When I was eight, I lived in a home where my mom was overwhelmed by the demands of raising three children. So I learned to be independent and never bother her. At the same time, my body was betraying me, giving me strange thoughts and "bad" desires. I adapted by disassociating from my body, floating at a thousand feet and watching life unfold. I believe this defense of becoming a mind at a distance, rather than a soul in a body, turned me into a writer. I am grateful for that. But it also severed me from my emotions. From knowing my body. From the right to have needs.

This I have come to believe: If we don't examine ourselves—our walls and defenses and blind spots—in the daylight and out in the open, we run the risk of a shutdown. What is buried will rise up and take over.

We must dig around under our houses and shore up the ground floor of our thinking, making it as sturdy as it can be. Not with answers, but with a way of looking actively at our world. We must invite our consciousness into full awareness of itself. To be astonished that we are alive, and aware of it, and wonder what it all means.

We can do this by thinking about the most important things in life.

In these pages, I have compiled eight elements that I believe form the foundation of who we are. The way we think about ourselves, the people in our lives, our relationships, and our homes affects everything else. Until we know ourselves, the language of our gut and spirit, we will continue to expect wrong things and misunderstand our motives. Misery is in direct proportion to expectation. And getting comfortable with this mystery of self, with the great unfolding of our lives, is the biggest step we can take toward existential joy. The death of anxiety. The embrace of the "why" behind all of our doing.

Some of what you'll read are essays I've written specifically for the book. Others are thoughts I've collected over the past five years and published in spurts elsewhere, online and in magazines. (Indeed, the idea of this book came when readers asked me to put my online writing in one physical place.) Some are snippets and thought-sparkers, meant to be read on a fifteen-minute subway ride. Others are longer and meant to be read under the covers on a slow Saturday morning. You'll find an evolution, a bit of "working it out" over several years in these pages. I am trying to be that friend who sits with you until three A.M., talking in swirls like milk poured in coffee.

We are not thoughtless lizards. As much as a blank mind would calm our twisted senses, it is not on offer. What we have are complex thoughts, spiritual meditations, and brains that want to hold the universe in our consciousness. This is the miracle of being human. If there is no God, and we are just atoms bouncing through a giant something, then the mystery of consciousness is all the more amazing. We are pieces of matter, perfectly organized in such a way that we are able to see ourselves. What an honor. What a commission. And if the saints and mystics are right, and we really are children of God, then wow. We are creations of the Most High, main characters in the cosmic drama of meaning. Maybe those two options aren't as different as we think.

This is my attempt to lean into the duty of consciousness. What we have are complex feelings, spiritual naggings, and brains that want to hold the universe in our consciousness.

Like
Streams
to the
Ocean

Ego

When we try to pick out anything by itself, we find it
hitched to everything else in the Universe.

—JOHN MUIR

My friend Lauren cofounded a nonprofit called Kind
Campaign. She travels to schools around the country and
speaks with young girls about bullying, unhealthy friendships, and identity. She looks younger than she is, she is styl-
ish, and she is beautiful. This piques the girls' attention, that
she is some strange creature who is adult and cool, yet young
and definitely not a teacher. At these talks, Lauren shares her
story of being bullied in seventh grade and how it spiraled
her into a severe depression and suicidal state. She teaches
the girls that sometimes it's hard to see outside their school
hallways. How, even though it feels like school is their entire
world, it's important to realize it's one chapter of their story.
That there's beauty, friendship, adventure, and so much life
lying ahead of them. And to know that when they are strug-
gling with things that feel big and scary, they can reach out
for help. That no one has to suffer alone.

She once told me a story of a high schooler who was
kicked out of her friend group and forced to get something
like one hundred likes on each Instagram post and some

ghastly number of new followers each day before she could sit with the other girls at lunch. This girl was so distraught, she told Lauren that she spent all her free time after school making fake accounts so that she could like her own posts and follow herself. "I have to do it," she said. "I'm miserable, but I have no choice."

Lauren hears endless stories like this—stories of brokenness, of girls confused and lost and trapped and scared.

Recently, a twelve-year-old came up to Lauren after the assembly. The girl was tiny, holding her hands down in front of her, making herself as small as possible as she gathered the strength to speak. "Can I ask you a question?" she mumbled.

Lauren leaned down. "I'm sorry—what, my darling?"

"Can I ask you a question?"

"Of course," Lauren said, now squatting to make herself smaller than the girl.

"Is it okay if I don't know who I am?"

Lauren gave her a look of understanding. Her heart broke at the baldness of the girl's honesty. She gave herself a second to think of an answer.

"It's perfectly fine to feel like you don't know yourself," she said finally. "One of the most beautiful parts of life is getting to know yourself over time, and that can change during different chapters of your life, too. I am still getting to know myself."

"You are?" the young girl said.

"Yes, I am. I know a lot about myself at this age. I like myself. But there is so much more to know. You are on a wonderful journey. You're exactly where you should be."

"Okay. Are you sure?"

"Yes, I'm sure."

The girl gave Lauren a half smile and stiffly hugged her. "Okay, thank you," she said, matter-of-factly.

What if I don't know "who" I am? There are layers in that girl's question. So much of life is lived in magnetic attraction to undefined concepts. Love. Meaning. Fulfillment. We all want to be somebody. But what is a somebody?

When I look back at my nervous journal entries, old photos, and confessions from high school and college, I see a through line. Every time I've been in a state of flux, of change, I fear that I will be trapped there. "Will this confusion last forever?" I wonder. But it never does, and I haven't grown weary yet in this business of uncovering, unmasking, and constructing who I am. It is both discovery and intention. And it is endless. And it's okay.

Yes, I'm sure.

"Who" you are is the braided marriage of circumstance, ego, and soul, in that order. First you have circumstance, the "what" of your life. Where you were born. Your sex and gender. Your parents and your hair and your skin and bones. The ego knits this all together into a whole, a concept. It is what most of us would consider "who" we are. The container in which you build an identity and then defend it. The ego acts as your agent, manager, and lawyer, all while believing it is the thing itself. Its worst fear is to be belittled or unnoticed. It takes everything personally.

Your body walks into a party where you don't know anyone. You feel anxious. That "you" is your ego. But another part of you is watching you get anxious. Something separate, but still you, is observing your ego, some higher part of you that says, "Why do I feel like this? Everyone seems so nice." This is your soul. We've all done something mad or wild and said, "Who am I right now?" This is the division between the ego and the soul. The ego's desires are based on the body, on scarcity and fear and lust and hunger. The soul's desires are based on . . . well, what does the soul want? Completion? Balance? Understanding? Acceptance? It's hard to know.

How strange is it that we're all walking around with this crowd in our head: our body; our ego, which is the mind of the body; and our soul, which is the watcher, the cosmic something else. Maybe it's nothing but a side effect of consciousness. But I am writing this right now, and I am also watching myself write it. Some part of me is above it, eternal, and cannot be hurt by failure or disgrace. What a nice part of me to seek out and cultivate.

We are three things. The car, the driver, and the awareness of it all.

I remember kissing a boy and experiencing all three parts. The sensation of touch and his weight on me. Of hands flying everywhere. I remember my ego paying close attention to how I was coming across. "Is my kiss right? Too much tongue? Not enough maybe? Is my hand okay here? Or does it seem like I'm swimming? Oh god. Okay, now every time I do something with my tongue, he does the exact same thing. Is he copying me? Maybe he's nervous, too?" And then the soul awareness coming from above. "Look at yourself. Aren't you funny, flailing on someone else as they flail on you. This is adorable. You're doing great, sweetie."

· · ·

I THINK MOST people live the majority of their lives in ego. Defined by what they're doing, what they're thinking, how they organize and categorize the world. I do what makes me comfortable, and avoid what makes me insecure. That pretty much sums up my life.

I don't like team sports. I have tragic hand-eye coordination and end up costing my team games. They laugh and say, "We're just out here having fun! Doesn't matter!" but I watch their eyes flare up in those moments of competitive adrenaline. They want to win. They love the animal thrill of victory, and I'm holding them back. So I avoid them. I tell them I don't like getting dirty or that I have work to do. Inside, it brings up the shame I felt when I was soft and slow as a child. My ego chimes in: "This will embarrass you. Instead of trying, tell your friends sports are dumb. Call them 'trite' and 'meaningless.' Focus on other sources of esteem."

This is also why I don't like going to clubs, the kind where single people go to look cute and dance. It's very lookie-loo and sexy, and I don't fit in. I'm not an Adonis, and I don't have good hair. Some of my friends love going. Dancing, getting hit on by strangers—it's a lighthearted thrill for them. They know I hate it, though, so they complain about it to make me feel included. "Ugh, another guy wouldn't leave me alone. I was like, dude, I'm here with my friends."

And I'll play along. "People are so desperate. I'm like, chill, let us live!" Of course, no one is ever hitting on me. But if I act annoyed, too, I can gather scraps of superiority.

I do like parties, though. I am good at talking, and people like my jokes. I meet new people and they laugh loudly and ask where I've been hiding all these years. Some of my

friends don't like these parties. They feel clumsy and insecure when talking to new people. A party of strangers is
exhausting for them. I'll walk away from a cackling stranger
and complain to my friend standing alone, "This random
person thinks I'm going to save their number in my phone
and hang out. That's cute." I say this to make my friend feel
special. They laugh with me. "People are clueless," they say.

I wonder how much of who we are comes down to doing
what we know we're good at, and avoiding what makes us
feel small. How far can we peel back the onion before our
personalities are just equations and chemical reactions? Perhaps if we really knew what made us feel small, we would
see that it had no business running our life.

INTERVIEWER: "What do you dislike most about your
appearance?"
ZADIE SMITH: "I like it all. Self-hatred is for younger,
prettier women."

—*Vanity Fair*

I'm glad I'm not too young or too pretty. When I was
young, I was an awkward blob. I had acne all over my face,
to the point where I couldn't rest my forehead on the desk at
school without pain. (This is something I often wanted to
do. Put my head down and shut out the world.) I ate BBQ
chips and Rocky Road ice cream and drank a six-pack of Dr
Pepper every day. Every day. By ninth grade, I weighed 190
pounds at five foot eight. And not in a cute teddy bear kind
of way. I looked like I was inflated haphazardly. With a thin
face and huge hips. It was almost like life decided to protect

me from vanity during the years when my mind and identity were forming.

I don't like extremes. They're a lonely, mutating force when entangled with the ego. Too pretty and you'll feel like a product. Everyone will want you, which you'll love at first, because youth wants attention and hormones want touch. But as you form into a whole person, you'll begin to wonder if your ideas and heart are as valuable as your face and body.

The same goes for other traits. Too clever, and you'll wield your words to control other people and feed your baser needs. You'll run the room and run your own head and let yourself off too easy when you're due a proper rebuke. Too rich, and your friends will feel inadequate. Too silly and you'll become a jester, a caricature. You won't trust your own sadness or awe. Too serious and you'll wrinkle and rust, unable to find the comedy in death and injustice. You'll have no stamina for the fight.

I want to be balanced like a year in Tennessee. A good winter that never gets too cold. A hot summer that drives me to the water. A neon-green spring and a crisp fall.

I want to like how I look, but not too much. Catch myself in the mirror and say, "Hey, not too bad. I like your hat."

FEW THINGS ARE trickier for the ego than good looks, money, and fame. One of our basest desires is to belong, and these "gifts," in abundance, complicate the search.

If you have one or a few of these things, you probably know what I'm talking about. Someone approaches you for your beauty or wealth, and you recognize their motive straight away—or, worse, miss the motive until it's too late.

Some people envy you. And if you struggle, you do not receive sympathy, because our culture has convinced us that people with these things should not have problems.

I have an acquaintance who is a billionaire. One of those tech guys who made ghastly amounts of money in his twenties on servers, computer storage, or something like that. He's my age—that is, still pretty young—with a lovely wife and a beautiful, healthy child. And yet the money has deformed him. He is as insecure as his bank account is large.

A few years ago, he was getting eviscerated in the press for a lavish birthday party he'd thrown. The comment section of one article was a bloodbath. People called him tone-deaf and disgusting and opulent. He was devastated. He had been a nerd his whole life, and his brilliance and hard work and luck had made him one of the richest people on the planet. Before he was rich, his friends had admired him for his mind. Now he was being mocked. I'll never forget him saying, "No one feels sorry for a billionaire." That one sentence had so much in it. Deep down, we believe money must solve our problems. As if we all think, "If I had that money, I'd be *set*. All my shitty problems would be gone. Why should *that* idiot have it?"

Since that party, the billionaire has dedicated hundreds of millions of dollars to an environmental charitable foundation that bears his name. He wants to solve the climate crisis. He wants to be remembered well. Perhaps one day his foundation will invent the clean energy source that saves this planet. All because an insecure kid was made fun of, and he tried to buy the love of the world by saving it.

We think we know what we want. But we're fooling ourselves. We do not understand the true nature of things.

. . .

I GOT B's in high school and a handful of A's. I was lazy as hell; smart enough to do the bare minimum and friendly enough with the teachers to get graded on a curve.

I always used to say, "If I tried, I could get all A's." In truth, I was afraid of failure. Of trying harder and ending up with the same grade, and knowing without a doubt that I couldn't do it. It was so much safer believing in the "maybe" than knowing the "no." That's one of the reasons I didn't like sports. I didn't like how it quantified things. The runner in the next lane is faster than you, by a lot. The numbers don't lie. Being a silly weirdo wasn't like that. No one sat around with a whistle, grading jokes and declaring winners of wit. To this day, I fear quantification. I would hate to know my IQ.

Zelda Fitzgerald said it like this: "I hope I'll never get ambitious enough to try anything. It's so much nicer to be damned sure I could do it better than other people." As you get older, though, you look around the world and see that avoidance doesn't do much. Sure, it keeps you from a little embarrassment here and there. But all the people I look up to, the artists and the athletes, the chefs and the CEOs, they risked embarrassment. . . . There was a moment when each of them stepped toward the fright. They applied for the job even if they knew it was a stretch. They told people of their coming glory. They asked the boy out. They sat down and wrote the book.

I keep learning these lessons, however reluctantly. However embarrassingly. Each day, I peel away a piece of armor that I built in eighth grade. I must have put a lot on.

. . .

WHEN I WAS a kid, someone asked me why I talked like a girl. I hated my voice for the next decade.

Later, when I was a teenager, a random kid walked up to me at school and asked why my acne was so bad. I said I didn't know why. "You need a dermatologist," he said. "Okay," I replied, with the awkwardness of a thousand puberties. But I never followed his advice. Seeing a doctor would have forced me to admit it was real. I had wished so badly to be invisible, I convinced myself that people couldn't see my face. But they could.

There are moments, especially in those early years, that become the structural support beams for our lives. We aren't born into a self. It is created without our consent. We build ourselves on top of comments, offhanded insults, inadequacies. By the time we wake up to ourselves, we are a Jenga stack of experiences that we spend the rest of our lives deconstructing. Sometimes I wonder what happened to God when he was young, to make him jealous enough to give us death. Perhaps it was the apple, the rejection. Maybe he was hurt.

This is happening to the young people in your life right now. Your kids. Your nephews and nieces. Your little siblings. We should be careful with the young people in our lives. Say kind things. Aspirational things. But also, go back and talk to yourself, unpack those moments. The thing someone said in eighth grade, that shook you forever? They probably didn't mean it. Maybe they don't even remember it.

Every time I've had the thrill of epiphany, it always comes as a new way of seeing what was already there. The knot in my stomach untangles. The experiences of life, which fell on me like chaos, reveal themselves to be lumber. Building materials for the life I was made to live.

I think we can forgive ourselves. We can forgive our parents. We can forgive God. We can say thank you for pain, because on top of it rests other blocks of companionship, of triumph and joy. We can say thank you because we don't really understand anything, and yet here we are.

We wake up atop the dirt of our childhoods with a shovel in our hands. In our pockets is a crumpled note with conspicuously familiar handwriting. It says, "Good luck."

I'VE BEEN THINKING about the hundreds of traits that affect how we move through the world. Beauty. Ethnicity. Charisma. Family. Economic privilege. Zip code. Physical abilities. You know those huge mixing boards in recording studios, with sliders and knobs to turn this sound up, that one down, to find the perfect mix? That's how I see all of us.

I think of my own mix: a gay, white, Christian boy from Tennessee. A kid with a soft body and acne. Teenage hotness? That knob is turned down. But a nice smile? Tick up the hotness just a little. Throw in a quick mind that adjusted to rejection by learning how to be funny, and a natural optimism that colors my humor playful instead of cold and cutting. A feminine voice? I had it, but got mocked for it, so I turned that knob down myself. I grew up with divorced parents and a family constantly in flux. Stability—middle position. Adaptability—turned up. But my parents loved me unconditionally and supported me in absolutely every way. Self-worth—turned up.

The traits play off one another and become something greater than their sum. Beauty is nice, but if you lack social skills, are depressed, or have been abused, life can still be hell. Or perhaps you could have a lot of societal dials turned against you—female, poor, black in the Deep South, a survivor of rape (for example, Oprah)—but have your discernment, intuition, charisma, smarts, ambition, and mastery of language turned all the way up. In an individualistic society like the United States, those qualities are practically religious virtues. Add to that our love for rags-to-riches stories, and that poor girl grows up to become a god.

A gay man like me, who was able to hide by changing his voice and body language pretty early on, is different from another who couldn't do that. We are both gay, and therefore share internal scripts that others don't . . . but there is not a perfect overlap. This is true for any person who finds themselves part of a group. They fit with their peers in one way, but the unique position of various sliders in their life prevents perfect matching. In every category you're put in, you can feel tremendous solidarity and isolating uniqueness at the very same time.

I SURPRISE MYSELF all the time. I'll be in a mood and want to go home, without knowing why. I'll drive home dreaming of a restful afternoon, but when I get there, I'll feel restless and hollow, somehow both tired and anxious to be doing something else. The same thing happens in my relationships.

I'll adore someone, and then for no reason start finding them frustrating. Something in me is watching that and saying, "Jed, why are you being a little bitch? Quit that." But I can't.

Which voice is the real me? The watcher or the actor?

Sometime last year, I was walking down the street with my friend Jordan, whistling. I said, "Jordan, think about whistling. I have no idea how my lips are making these tiny movements to hit the exact next note of the Mario theme song. The movement is so tiny I can't even imagine it, and yet my lip muscles know what to do." We spent the rest of the walk making observations like this. "I have no idea how I'm walking right now. I don't know how my legs are moving. They just are." We laughed at our ignorance. At the marvel of being alive and able to move and do things.

I feel my best when I forget myself, my body, my existence. When my self-conscious drive to name and label falls asleep. I am just a weed in the field, loving the breeze and eating the sun. I don't know what I am.

I'VE HAD PEOPLE see me driving alone—maybe they'd stopped in town at a red light, and noticed me in the car next to them—and say, "Jed! You looked so sad. What was wrong?" I wasn't sad; I was just alone in my car and thinking. Or maybe not thinking. Just driving and being simple. Should I be grinning to myself in the car? No.

Those encounters made me realize how communicative our faces are, how we expect that they be "on" whenever we're around people. Alone and in a neutral state, our faces take a stillness that would be interpreted as sadness or anger in the company of another. Makes me wonder how much personality is put on. How different we'd act if alone too long.

YOU KNOW WHEN it's dark outside, and the lights are on in a house across the street? You can see in the kitchen, and the mom is there and she's doing dishes or something. Or maybe it's not the mom. It could be the mistress, and the mom is away on a work trip. Maybe it's a roommate. How can I know? But I do this all the time. I'll notice a neighbor doing things in the window, and make up an entire story about who they are.

Somehow, the more people crammed together in a place, the easier it is to be alone. To not know who's across the way, living their life. I'm never more alone than when I'm on an airplane, touching knees with a stranger, headphones on.

You may meet me and then think that you know me. I am an open book, so your guesses will often be right. But the lights are on at night, and your guesses are only guesses. There are rooms inside of me that don't face the street. There are kids playing in the basement. There are cars in the driveway. At best, we're all guessing.

I once asked a friend, as a kind of test: "When you meet someone new, do you automatically trust them until they prove they shouldn't be trusted? Or do you treat everyone as suspect, and make them prove that they are worthy?"

He said, "I assume they're annoying and terrible, and they have to prove to me that I'm wrong."

I laughed. "I am the opposite. I assume they're great and a future friend. They have to prove to me that they're terrible."

"This is why you suffer so many fools," he said.

"Or why I have so many friends."

What do you see in the window? What do you assume?

"IN TEN YEARS, none of this is going to matter." Older people would tell me that in high school, when I was all torn up about a friendship. They would say it when I was stressed beyond belief in college, embroiled in roommate drama or writhing in unrequited love.

People in their thirties, fresh out of the madness of adolescence, love to say things like that. To pat the youngsters on the head and say, "I remember when I was all hormones and no chill; it'll pass." Often, these thirtysomethings are saying it to themselves more than anyone else. They're congratulating themselves for surviving.

But to the high schooler, the college sophomore, it matters now. It is life or death.

And really, it does matter. The drama is testing our social skills. Teaching us to read the signals of jealousy, hurt, sarcasm, and betrayal. Our fights and crushes and gossip are the emotional muscles flexing, in the same way a baby flails her arms and legs in the crib to see how far they stretch. To build those baby muscles. Soon enough, to stand.

We feel too much in those years. We jam our hearts into every glass slipper.

We can't become wise without living first. We can't know peace without chaos first. We can't know belonging until we've hedged our bets on the wrong clan and felt alone in a crowded room.

"It won't matter in ten years" is untrue. It all matters. It just won't feel like it feels now. For some, it'll transform from panic into gratitude, from scarcity into strength. But this doesn't happen for everyone. Some people build themselves on their pain. It defines them. Perhaps the pain is so big that it should. But for most of us, the felt transgressions of growing older and bumping into other people are an invitation to growth. It matters how we frame it.

So MUCH MENTAL energy is spent maintaining self-worth. When an artist makes something, and God forbid it is a success, a new horror is born: "Will I ever make something this good again? Will anyone care? Was it an accident?" The fear always returns to you. To your idea of yourself. To how you think you're coming across. And the mysterious, made-up projection of how you think others think of you.

I glance at the mirror and think I look pretty good. Then I see a photo of myself and I look like a bridge troll. Same day. Same clothes. Somehow the mirror allows me to shapeshift in my imagination. To trick myself or something. But the picture says otherwise. Maybe because it's static, and in the mirror I can wiggle until I like an angle. I'll see the photo and say, "Do I really look like that?" And my friend will say, "Yes, you look great. What are you talking about?"

I've seen people modify photos of their faces so severely that they look like a different person online. Smoothed out, cartoonish, and plastic. "Surely they are making a joke," I think. But they are not. And I wonder what their blindness to their own face means. And what blind spots I have.

I know some of the stories I've made up to maintain my

self-worth. As a kid, I highlighted my weirdness and uniqueness to remove myself from competition. I memorized Stanley Kubrick movies. I watched anime. I wrote poems and bought movie soundtracks. I was obsessed with film composers like John Williams and Danny Elfman. This differentiated me from the jocks who loved the Red Hot Chili Peppers and watching baseball. I built my identity on untouchable things.

This way of being followed me into adulthood. I don't feel jealous of anyone. I don't compare myself to anyone. I like myself. My sense of identity is built in culture, and cleverness, in taste, in making a well-timed reference. But I also see how this part of me was built in the insecure halls of middle school. My insecurities, and my responses to them, shaped who I am today, a person I seem to like. A person who feels superior to those washed-up jocks with torn ACLs and beer bellies.

SING THE BODY

Sing the body,
What have I not hated about my own?
I remember joking in high school that
I would never procreate, to protect
the species from my ugliness.

I remember thinking my hands were handsome,
And my teeth were straight,
Measly concessions for a body
Meant for the basement.

But oh,
Sing your thirties,
When I stopped wishing I was someone else,
Two decades of that had scalded me.
And something switched.
The mirror stopped its hissing,
Its condescending remarks.
I stopped hating my skeleton, my skin, the way my body
    did what it needs to do.
This is my body, and it is good.
And sometimes, in romantic moments, I let people love
    it. And they do love it.
No matter how the buried teenage boy in me tries to
    warn them "You are being tricked! This is ugliness."
    No. It is not. It is the body of a man. And he carries
    it as a man.
How you sing the body is what your lover hears. Sing to
    yourself.
I've heard the song of the forties is even sweeter.

MY FRIEND TOM, a filmmaker, professor, and writer, told me, "Whatever your pain is, that's where you're going to find your passion. Whenever I talk to students, I ask them, 'Where do you hurt specifically?' For example, the school system always pushed me out. It didn't accept the creative person that I was, and nobody listened to me, so my passion now is listening to kids and accessing the voice in them that has been quieted and silenced. That came from my pain."

Look at how people give back. How they choose to help

the world. The rich donate to causes or start foundations. The middle class give what they can or spend time volunteering. Notice how they choose to put purpose in their life, how it almost always has a personal cause. They had a daughter with cystic fibrosis? They donate to research to cure it. They suffered police abuse and now rally in the streets for justice. The thing that injured you often becomes a piece of your purpose in life.

There are two privileges. The privilege of worldly access: the world being made for you, of wealth and whiteness and a runway of ease. And its opposite, the privilege of spiritual access: the world not being made for you, the forced awakening of the inner eye, the hard hand and invitation to see the world clearly. The first is a privilege that blesses you early and hurts you late. In the end, it robs you of the invitation to wisdom and harmony. The other hurts you early and blesses you in time.

My friend Téquan told me stories of how he got picked on in high school. Being called a faggot for his voice and mannerisms. He ran away from home and went wild to get away from it. Sex and drugs and all the staples of rebellion. He burned bright and hot. Then, at twenty-four, he had his great awakening and quit it all.

"In some ways, you're lucky," I said. "You were forced to face your real identity early. You had to test it and find it fast, because the world wasn't made for you. That's why you're so whole now, and still so young."

"Well, I do love who I am," he said, "but damn, it was a journey. But yeah, I guess I'm glad I'm not coming out only now, with a kid and a wife, or a broken-up heart and all confused as fuck."

Sometimes, the hurt from your youth is the horrible hand of God, refining you toward wisdom and purpose.

What stands in the way, becomes the way.

—Marcus Aurelius

As a kid, I was terrified of being called gay. I didn't want to be different. I didn't want to be described as "my gay friend Jed," but rather, "my friend Jed."

Being labeled is claustrophobic. It locks you into connotations. And so I hid. I tried to change my voice. Talk less with my hands. Be funnier. Sharp and clever. My first goal was to belong. And because I looked like all my friends, all I had to do was change my behavior.

I think about this a lot when I consider the lives of people of color in a white majority. Where I could disappear behind behavior in a straight majority, they cannot. The skin cannot hide.

Have you ever been dragged to a party where you didn't know anyone? You sit on the couch and feel the thickness in the air. "Do I belong? Do they wish I hadn't come?" It's not that people are outright mean to you. Maybe even the host comes to say hi. But in the middle of that conversation, you get a look from someone across the room that says, "Who is that guy?" You feel the eyes.

It's not just the outright bigotry. It's also the cool girl with the big house throwing a party. She would never say, "No black people, no gays." That would feel mean and set off the alarms of conscience. It's more, "Do I know you? Do we have things in common?" The unseen biases. The selective attraction to the "similar," which is much more common than conscious rejection.

That is just it. I feared being rejected so I tried to morph into the majority. I lowered my voice. I sharpened my sense of humor so that I could deflect a comment or win the crowd. If you are different, and most teenagers feel different in one way or many, you contort yourself to fit in. And it takes years of untangling your limbs to become wholly you. Now, I carry my otherness with swagger. What was once a cancerous growth on my identity, is now a badge, a prize. I see this in so many communities of "otherness." They start in the shadow of loneliness, of rejection, and find one another, and band together and begin to radiate a light of their own making. But what is the cost?

I wonder what a lifetime of feeling "other" would do to me—if my tricks of behavior hadn't made me friends—if my sexuality had lead to true rejection. I wonder what a million cuts of bias do to our friends. I bet I would be angry. A hum of rage behind my eyes. I think growing up "other" gave me thick skin, and I think we should all have thick skin. But a tender touch now and then can bring me to tears.

I CAN'T GET this out of my head: When I bullshit someone, they don't care. I'm bullshitting myself. The lie lives on in me.

When I pretend to be less or more than my full identity, I present a character to the world. One I must maintain and prune and reinvent and defend. I poison my authenticity by the acrobatics of personal propaganda, propping up the idiot dictator of my ego. Spending my time imagining what other people are thinking instead of thinking for myself.

The parts of me I hide are an implicit judgment: This part of me is bad. This part is not good enough. I am ashamed. And shame is a flesh-eating disease.

I want coherence. I want the through line to be visible. I don't want anyone to dig up a part of me and play "gotcha." What a tense way to live.

A GUY I went on a few dates with once texted me: "I sold my Coachella tickets."

"Why? I thought you were so excited!" I wrote. We had connected over loving music festivals.

"I got a pimple," he said.

"Lol," I wrote back. "For real did you sell them? Why?"

"I told you, I got a zit on my chin. I don't look cute. I'm not going."

I cannot tell you how flabbergasted I was. What in the world? How can someone care about their appearance that much?

After a vicious cycle of mocking this person in my head, I received a tender thought. *Everyone just wants to bring something to the table.*

The vain person, refining the angle of their face for the camera, staying home because of a zit. They fear that if their look is off, people will say, "Why are they here?"

The comedian, speaking louder now to make sure the joke lands, making fun of the vain person, mocking everything in a frenzy. He fears that if he doesn't get laughs, people will say, "Why is he here?"

The relationship wizard, asking about boys and girls you have kissed, talking about hearts and entanglement. They fear that if they don't have their finger on the gossip, on the up-to-date *who* and *where,* people will ask, "Why are they here?"

I wonder if we'd feel insecure on a desert island. I know I wouldn't worry about my hair. My jokes. I wouldn't care to keep up with the news. I wouldn't have to compile my cleverness for the dinner table tonight. Would the feeling of contentment last? I would probably play with a hermit crab for the afternoon, and tell him how lovely his claws were. Pretty soon, I'd hope he liked me. Approved of me. Crawled to me tomorrow.

MY FRIEND'S NEWBORN was crying. She picked up her baby. "What's wrong, my love? Are you hungry?" Nope. She wasn't hungry. "Maybe your diaper is ready for changing? Oh, there it is." She changed the diaper and, just like that, the baby stopped crying. She said, "My doula helped me reframe it all. She said, 'Your baby isn't crying. She's talking. She just doesn't know any words yet. So she's doing the best she can to communicate.'"

She's not crying, she's talking.

Babies cry because they can't speak. They don't know how to ask for what they need. They might not even know *what* they need. So they wail. The nag of a mystery craving is madness.

When adults can't speak to their discontent, when they

can't quite figure out what it is they're wanting, they will try anything. They drink or commit adultery or quit their jobs or run away or live vicariously through their kids or stonewall their husbands. They knock things off the counter just to feel some control. They burn down their own house to escape it, without really knowing where else to go.

This is the tragedy of being an animal with a mind. We are punching the walls to stop the ache in our chest.

THE OTHER DAY, a friend of mine drank too much and said some nasty things. Dark and hateful. Not about me, but about another friend. And I was shocked. I thought he liked this person. Actually, he'd said lovely things about them at dinner earlier that night. But now he was going on and on about how they're "shit and talentless and cheap."

I was sober enough to protest, and to know that my friend wouldn't remember saying this the next day. But it sent me into a spin as I went to bed. I've always agreed with the saying "I don't trust anyone who doesn't drink, because I don't know who they really are." People show more of their inside minds when loosened by alcohol. But with this friend, I was frightened to think that his outburst was the "real him." That deep down, he was hateful and bitter, and the surface was a mask.

I got some good advice about this when I brought it up with another friend. They told me, "We're all insecure and dealing with lots of layers. Maybe a few drinks take away his inhibition, and you see into who he is . . . but too drunk is another story. Don't worry about it. Your friend probably suffers from some insecurities about taste and career. Him getting nasty doesn't mean he is a nasty person. We all have that in us. He should just be careful when he drinks."

WHEN I WAS a kid watching the Golden Globes, one of the celebrities on the red carpet said, "I just ran into Brad Pitt at the urinal! He was standing next to me . . . peeing!"

I thought, "Whoa . . . Brad Pitt goes to the bathroom? Who knew?"

Why would that be a surprise? No one has ever told me that the rich and famous don't use the bathroom. I came up with that on my own. Why?

Perhaps Barack Obama gets toe cramps and dribbles a little extra after he pees. George Clooney has gone to the toilet and realized, too late, that there's no toilet paper. Meryl Streep has taken off her shoes on the couch and realized her feet smell like death, and that her friends must smell them, too.

It must have something to do with our delusion that money and fame remove the embarrassments of being human. They must solve our basic problems.

When I was little, I wanted to write a fan letter to a Disney animator who had worked on *Aladdin*. His name was Eric Goldberg. My hero. My mom said, "I'll find his address." I protested: "Mom, I can't just write him. He's famous!"

"Jed, everyone is a human being," she said. "Everyone. And they all love to be encouraged."

So I wrote Eric Goldberg a letter and my mom sat on the phone like a private eye tracking down his address.

A month later, he wrote back. He drew me an original

drawing of the Genie that said, "Yo, Jed, I ain't never had a friend like you." I was ten years old.

From that moment, I've always believed I could talk to anyone.

People are people. No more, no less. And they all love to be encouraged.

MY FRIEND'S UNCLE once told me, "I wouldn't have any idea how old I was if I didn't own a mirror. I'm fifty-five, but I still feel twenty-five. I quit looking at mirrors last year."

That was years ago, but I still think about it. We are so aware of what we look like.

Without mirrors and photography, I wouldn't really know how my face appears to other people. I guess a calm puddle would give me a clue, but those aren't terribly common in Southern California. For ninety-five percent of our species' history, we had only puddles.

How many times have I had a fun time dancing at a birthday party, then when someone shows me a video from that night, I see my ugly-ass dance moves for what they are? Immediately, I am horrified, worried what people were "really" thinking about me. The freedom and joy I felt then is erased by the shame I feel now. I wish I'd never seen myself.

"PRECARIOUS MANHOOD"—A BETTER term for Toxic Masculinity—might be the most destructive force in society. The tender boy falls prey to the teenage years, when the world tells him to lock away his emotions and treat sincerity as a joke. In high school, I can't tell you how many times a moment of male encouragement or kindness degenerated into "no-homo" jokes or hyper-homo mockery.

Human beings are a cocktail of masculinity and femininity. To believe that we are meant to emulate one pole at the expense of the other, and that our sex alone should tether us to a caricatured extreme, is scientifically false and destructive. We all know masculine women and feminine men. One out of a thousand people are born intersex.

We are alchemy, not static elements.

And when we fight the truth to imitate a cartoon, of course we suffer. These boys suppress their complexity and hurt and affection, and coil up into dangerous springs of misplaced energy. They become presidents, CEOs, husbands. They wage wars and punch their spouses. Their companies destroy nature because a multifactored co-dependent ecosystem is something incomprehensible to them. Because the balance of femininity is denied them, total compartmentalization is the norm. Looking at the world one way and blocking out the effects of all the others.

The word "masculinity" almost has a dirty connotation to me. In childhood, it was a word used as a weapon against "sissy boys" and artists. It came to mean most of the things I dislike in men. Blind strength. Bullying. Boasting. Hierarchy built on things I didn't possess.

Until men understand their own hearts, until we make room for the bigness of one another, we will continue to suffer.

I don't know if it's a masculine trait or a trait expressed

by all humans equally, but some men have a unique ability to walk away from personal failure. At least, this is what I've seen in some of the men around me. It must be related to compartmentalization. They can wake up in the trash of their own life—in a room turned upside down, with the drapes on fire—and become as calm as a surgeon. They walk out the front door and never look back.

I've seen fathers, boyfriends, friends get so tangled in their mistakes and shame that their only recourse seems to be a total reset. Their pride becomes a dead-eyed shark. The hard work of analyzing their life, of parsing out what went wrong and setting out to fix it, is too great, too close to damning their idea of who they are. To fix a deformed leg, sometimes you must first break the bone and set it right. They won't have it. It is better to limp away. And they do it without a wince on their face.

I met a man in Baja California who left his life in Texas to start fresh. He said he'd had a family, but it "got complicated," so he left. Now, in his sixties, he lives on the beach in a camper van.

When I spent two summers in Alaska as a teenager, I remember seeing the same thing. There were so many grizzled men with wrinkles acquired from wrongdoing. They came to Alaska to forget and to be forgotten. The state seemed full of them. Patagonia is like that, too. The ends of the earth. The places that do not ask follow-up questions.

I know I have it in me. In a small, frightening way, I have felt it when I've failed and my soul hardens like a statue. I've felt a surge of shame flip some switch and turn me cold. Meticulous. Surgical.

I won't live like that. It takes a safe and wide love to teach a man that it's possible to fail and remain.

WHEN OUR CULTURE finds a healthy understanding of masculinity and femininity, and how these two energies coexist in all of us, we will see big changes in mental health. Men won't silence their tenderness for fear of emasculation. Women won't squash their power for fear of being effemulated. "Effemulation" isn't a word, but how interesting that there isn't an equivalent of "emasculation" in the feminine, as if the masculine is so vulnerable to corruption that it needed a special word.

In middle school, I remember seeing drag queens in high heels and thinking, "They are so annoying. I'm not gay like them!" What I had done was internalize homophobia as a survival mechanism. If I made fun of "those" gays, maybe I would be more masculine and therefore safer in my straight world. And, indeed, I was rewarded for it. I had straight friends who would introduce me by saying, "He's gay but not THAT gay."

In my midthirties, I am still unpacking the big-ass suitcase of fears and insecurities and blind spots that I discovered in adulthood.

So I am leaning in to living it. I don't judge my voice any more. I don't wonder if I'm speaking with my hands too much. I don't worry that someone can tell I'm gay. I don't say disparaging things about any form of gender manifestation. I want to embody freedom so that others might be free. I want to be a true man, both feminine and masculine, to let my adolescent self know that not only is it okay, it is the only truth there is.

WHENEVER SOMEONE IS freaking out over nothing . . . when their world has come undone because she won't text back, or the airline lost their luggage, or they got another parking ticket . . . I want to point to the sky and say, "Um, we're floating on a boulder in space, spinning at an incredible speed, held down by gravity and some arbitrary rule of physics. There's only so much organic material on this planet, which means we're made of molecules that came from dead stars. Dead. Stars. Some part of you was probably part of a dinosaur. For you to exist, every single one of your ancestors had to survive long enough to procreate, all the way back to the Stone Age and monkeys and small mammals and reptiles and fish and cells. You exist thanks to an unbroken chain of successful sex. Everything is a miracle . . . so calm your ass down."

I'm tempted to say all of that. But I usually just say, "Oh, man. Sorry about all that. Want a LaCroix?"

WHEN CHANGE IS due, your gut knows first, followed by the mouth, then the head. If a relationship is toxic, we will feel it and complain about it long before we know it's over. We will betray ourselves with our words. Our friends will tell us this. Our brains are the last to know.

When you know something is not true, it becomes increasingly more difficult to defend it. Whether it's your bad relationship, your ego, your gender identity, or destructive traditions. Your head will rage against the dying of the light, because the devil it knows is better than the devil it doesn't. Meanwhile, your gut is prepping the room with balloons and cake, waiting for you to show up to the surprise of peace and good sleep.

Each human life is like a winding, narrow path through the woods, sometimes moving uphill, sometimes down, sometimes doubling back from a dead end. But our species as a whole moves more like a glacier, carving through the mountains to make a way. The valley we leave will be a natural park someday, visited by tourists as a wonder of the world.

IN MY TWENTIES, I didn't know any married gay couples. I'm sure they were out there, but I didn't know where to find them. I was trying to grow up and be a man and love God and be good. I didn't want to be a scandal. I didn't want to be rejected by the only community I'd ever known. Loving who I wanted to love felt selfish. If being a Christian meant "Dying to self, and serving God," and the Bible said that being gay was wrong, then choosing to follow my heart instead of God was the most selfish thing I could do, I rationalized.

In truth, it just felt scary. I didn't want to lose my whole world in search of a kiss.

I remember thinking, "How come I can't find any committed gay couples who love God? Maybe they don't exist. And if they don't exist, maybe that explains why God warned against it." This line of thinking kept me single my entire twenties. Afraid of any kind of romantic love.

I needed examples. I wasn't built to go off on my own, spit in the face of my tradition. The saying from scripture,

"The heart is deceitful above all things," swirled in my head. My heart could be lying to me. What a curse.

One day, around the age of twenty-seven, I was telling all this to a kind and patient mentor of mine. I told him how I didn't have any examples, any lives to model mine after. I figured he'd tell me to trust God and pray to be healed. He didn't.

He said, "Jed, it can be hard to tell the difference between an outcast and a pioneer. What if you're meant to be the example you needed? What if God gave you your personality, your unique skill set, to equip you to walk into the wilderness and show that it can be done?"

I stared at him while the question expanded in my chest. I hadn't thought of it like that before.

"And trust me," he continued, "those examples are out there, just maybe not in your community. So look hard, read everything, pray, and move in the direction of what's right. God will correct your steps, but you must first start walking. That's what 'walk in faith' means."

My mentor didn't say it just like that. It was years ago and I'm sure my memory has embellished it. But that conversation changed my life. Just because you don't have a road map doesn't mean you aren't meant to walk in the direction of your convictions. Look at your gifts, your skills. You may be a pioneer.

A friend once said to me, "Most people are unhappy with their life. They're stuck in a situation that isn't what they hoped for, but they don't see a way out. And they don't see examples of freedom." That is it. We need models. We need examples of a way out.

Some of those lone wanderers in the desert are not outcasts. They're pioneers. They became the way out—first for themselves, and then for others. This goes for all manners of living. Of the job you want. Of the community you need. Of the project you fear to start. We are waiting for permission, for examples. But what if you are the example?

My views on how to feel safe in this world have expanded exponentially. For me, I kept opening doors with trembling hands and fists up ready for a fight. But the more I've done this, and found smiling faces behind the door, the safer I've felt in the endless halls of my constantly changing life. And the wildest thing is, when you think no one is modeling what you need, and you dare to step into that for yourself, you will find the room crowded with comrades, with bright eyes and high fives and "You, too?" It's the best feeling in the world. The feeling of God saying, "Hah, my love, you thought I was so small."

I WILL NEVER forget sitting on the couch with two of my roommates and asking them, "What's an insecurity that you have that I wouldn't know?" These are good friends of mine. Handsome men in their twenties. Loaded down with friends and cool jobs. They said, almost at the same time: "I fear that one day I'm going to wake up and realize that my friends have figured me out, that I'm not cool, and they're going to stop talking to me. I think about this every day." In a million tries, I could never have guessed that they would feel this way. And they both did.

Ten years after this conversation, one of those friends killed himself. He took his life this past summer. About five years ago, he moved away from California and stopped talking to most of us. Moved away and cut us out. Those of us left behind would talk about it, shocked and saddened. Guessing at his motives. Wondering how one of our favorite people could just discard his whole community. Maybe he had become more Christian, and considered us backsliders and pagans. Maybe his new friends turned him against us. We didn't know.

In the year since he died, I've thought often about his answer to that question. How he wondered if he was faking it, and if we would find out. If he thought we were faking it, too. He married a beautiful woman and had a child on the way. He was full of laughter and seemed to have a lovely life. And then he ended it. I don't know if his answer to that question all those years ago was a clue to what was coming, or just an insecurity that a lot of us share. I don't know if he had a freak moment of brain chemistry and maybe it had nothing to do with sadness at all. My mind turns it all over, the way we study a tragedy to prevent its repeating.

It shows how little we know about one another. Most people walk around with invisible strings. Fears about being liked, being enough, marriage, career, vanity, talent, belonging. If you could see the strings pulling at people, you'd be as patient as a pillow with everyone you met.

WHEN I SEE something good in someone, I tell them straight away. Like a reflex. Even if I don't know them at all. I am always telling waitresses how beautiful their hair is or how charming they are, or bartenders how masterful they are with the flip of a bottle.

This can often be mistaken for flirting. Maybe it is; I love flirting. But I've seen the effects of doing this, and I've felt its effects on me. A kind word can turn a glazed-over stranger into a bright-faced friend. As if they suddenly see themselves in the world, approved by a stranger they had previously ignored. I have found that a compliment from a stranger can reshape my day. And it matters that it is a stranger. If a random kid says he likes my jacket as I walk by, I feel like a fashion genius. If my buddy says it, I'm glad—but not as radiant and giddy as when the compliment comes from someone with no reason to be nice to me.

There is something about speaking lovely words to people. Our nervous minds are always trying to see themselves, to fish out the mystery of our standing in the world. Words have all the power. Have you noticed how when someone says, "My first impression of you was . . . ," you perk up with wild interest? We want to meet ourselves.

This phenomenon works the other way, too. In a moment of anger, an emotional pronouncement over someone can poison them for years. "You are a disappointment." "You are lazy." Saying what someone "is" is like witchcraft. It sticks to you like a spell. The statement may be true in a single moment—you may have been lazy today—but the saying of it can warp your future. "You were lazy today" transforms into "You *are* lazy." It can act like a curse.

For this reason, I tell people what is lovely, so that it becomes more of them. If a talkative friend stops and listens to me, I pause and say, "You're such a good listener." She might lean back and put her hand on her chest and say "I am?" And I'll say, "Yes, thank you." She'll be a better listener from that day on.

Words have power, to bless or to curse. That's why I love

reading them, writing them in cafés, hearing them and saying them. They shape the world.

ERIK ERIKSON WAS the developmental psychologist whose
work in the 1950s gave us the term "identity crisis." In your
teenage years, he said, you enter a crisis of "identity versus
role confusion." This is the crossroads of discovering your
passions, caring about what others think, fitting into a tribe,
and maintaining a sense of self. All these feelings collide in
high school, and the dust does not often settle until your late
twenties.

What's wild is that this sense of groping for identity is so
common, in spite of how unique and varied each life is. A
kid can have married parents, divorced parents, straight
parents or gay parents, be gay, straight, trans, Christian,
atheist, rich, poor . . . and will go through these phases, too.
Erikson points out that in the case of historical geniuses, the
discovering of "true identity" is often delayed. Toni Morri-
son's first book was published when she was thirty-nine.
Miguel de Cervantes wrote *Don Quixote* in his late fifties.
Cézanne had his first solo exhibition at fifty-six. That should
give some of us comfort. Maybe the reason we don't have
our shit together yet is because we're geniuses.

THERE'S SELF-WORK, AND then there's self-obsession. I love
personality tests like the Enneagram. I love how knowing
I'm a Type 7 tells me something about myself. That at my
core, I avoid pain. It's why I'm always traveling and finding
new adventures. It's why I jump from pain to laughter, from

hurt to cerebral understanding. Why I leave the room when someone is crying. It has helped me understand myself.

All this self-excavation is crucial for living a whole, embodied life. For understanding how I work and how I experience the world, how I am in relationships. But I don't want to get lost in it. I've too often reduced people to their Enneagram number. "You're such a three! That's why you whiten your teeth." I've seen people go to so many retreats, try every new thing, and read every new book. A frantic pattern that only walls the soul deeper behind a mountain of knowledge and lingo. Of performative self-understanding.

There's a balance. I don't trust someone who isn't interested in their own excavation. But I feel similar about people who overdo it, who are lost in the mirror maze of themselves. Whose every act is an act of self-analysis. There is no living in this scenario, only analyzing.

I want to be a conscious soul, curious about my makeup. I want to do the important work. But I also acknowledge that I am a strange animal, essentially unknowable to myself. And so are you. An honest wildling who is hungry and eats. A coyote who doesn't know too much for his own good.

THE IMAGE THAT returns to me most often is the journey of water. It is the most complete metaphor, the most comforting.

Water falls as snow on the mountains. As a trillion tiny bits without memory. The love of the sun transforms the snow. They melt and feel one urgency: gravity. They did not learn this. It is just mysteriously ever present. The stream starts small, a clear trickle. Uncluttered with the confusion of sediment or history, it rolls over rocks and joins with other newborn streams and widens. The beginning of a lifetime of widening.

On its way down the mountain, the stream becomes the creek. It collects soil and memories. It flattens a bit. It meets farms and bridges and other confusing things.

It joins with other creeks and becomes a river. It is brown now with soil and experience and runoff and living. It runs slower, no longer in a hurry. Muddy with patience, yet always feeling that pull, toward somewhere it is certain exists, but has never seen.

Finally, after a life that started as simply as a clear stream, it pours, wide as a mile, into the ocean, the endless breadth of eternity. The home it hoped for was real.

And the love of the sun is on the ocean. Its heat never stops, and before long, it breaks the water's surface into a trillion little nothings, lifting them like blank souls and sending them back to the mountain. First as rising evaporation. Then clouds. Then as snow. And we do it all over again. We come from an endlessness wider than the horizon. We are pulled to the sky to begin again, narrow and clear, and make our return.

Life is learning to ever widen.

Family

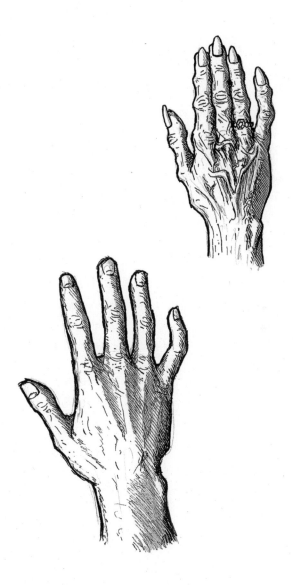

Imagine yourself at nine years old. Picture your world: your parents or lack of parents, your siblings, your home or lack of home. Did you feel safe? Noticed? Did you have to make your own way, or were you nurtured?

As I said before, this season in our lives—between eight and ten years old—is when "the self" turns on like a light. How you saw the world then is how you will likely see it for the rest of your life. It's the original coding on which all your other memories sit. You figured out how to be okay, how to behave in order to feel safe.

An example. At nine years old, I lived with a wonderful mother and a distant stepdad. I had a fun father and a stepmom who I saw on weekends. My dad and stepmom had an infant daughter, my little half sister. She was cute and innocent of all the family complexities of divorce. But the three kids my parents had while they were together, we were different. There was me; my older sister, the wild one; and my little brother, who was always dealing with medical issues. I saw how taking care of them devoured my mom's time and energy. I loved her and she loved me, but she had her hands full. So I decided to need nothing. I aimed to become good and invisible. I'd get good grades and play in the woods and do my own thing.

This compulsion to be independent and not disturb anyone worked its way into the core of my personality. To this day, I won't let anyone go to the doctor with me when I'm sick. I can't ask a favor. I'll do it on my own. And I'll be strong, never needy, never cumbersome. In romantic relationships, I don't think to ask for more affection, or better communication. The thought that I could be worthy of asking for something—of feeling things, founded or unfounded, and speaking them—is so far removed from my consciousness. That I could be hurting and ask for help. Wow. Even typing that is hard. I cringe.

There doesn't have to be a villain in a story like this. My parents loved and cared for me and gave me a fantastic childhood. Many kids are not nearly as lucky as I was. But you don't have to have shitty parents to inherit wrong thinking simply by circumstance. It's just the thorny way of life. This is everyone's story and everyone's duty: to reach adulthood and then do the hard work of unpacking your childhood, your family, the weapons you picked up to protect your little body.

ON THE JOURNEY of growing up, there are casualties. That nine-year-old kid is trying to survive. And if you had siblings, you may have stepped on a few necks to save yours. You may have said a mean word to feel in control. You may have hit or pushed someone to learn the impact of force. You're finding yourself, and you don't know what you don't know. It is hard to admit that you leave a wake behind you. It is hard to admit that you may indeed be someone else's villain.

I was horrible to my little brother, Luke. I tortured him. I enjoyed it. When I learned he was claustrophobic, I started sneaking up behind him with our giant beanbag chair and

leaping on top of him. I was twice his size. He would scream
a real, horror movie scream, and it thrilled me. I loved to
hear him scream. Sure, I knew I wasn't actually hurting him.
And that was part of the pleasure: that he was afraid for no
reason. That he sounded ridiculous. I loved the psychological terrorism.

Luke was never mean to me. He was and is pure kindness. He would come to watch television with me in the living room, and I would yell at him to get out. He would try
playing Nintendo with me and I would shake with rage. I
would walk in on him playing videogames and proclaim,
"You have five minutes and then it's my turn!"

We shared a room until I was about eleven or twelve. I
hated sharing with him. I got a roll of duct tape and made a
barrier down the center of the room. I even stood on a chair
and made it wrap all the way around the ceiling.

"This is my side of the room and that is yours. You do
not ever come on my side. None of your toys or things can
touch my side."

"But the door to the room is on your side. How do I get
out?"

"Through the window," I said.

I remember, even at that young age, wondering why I
hated him so much. In my calmer alone moments, I didn't
hate him. It was only when I saw him that the impulse came
alive.

My mom would referee our fights. "When y'all grow up,
you'll be friends," she would say. "You'll love each other.
That's how it always happens." We ignored her as we
punched and clawed. Him always in self-defense. I'm sure
he started it once in a while. But I know it was only a re-

sponse to my brutality. A chance to feel agency on his part for once.

In his early teens, Luke developed a stutter. His words stopped and started, and he struggled to finish sentences. I didn't think much of it. It occurred to me much later that the stutter might have been a response to me mocking him every time he opened his mouth.

In high school, we were a bit better. We fought less. We had our own rooms and went to different high schools. He had medical needs and had to go to a school with more individualized attention. Then one day, he said offhandedly, "I'm going to kill you when you turn thirty-two."

I laughed. He laughed.

"To pay you back for torturing me my whole life," he added.

I don't know why he chose thirty-two. But I remember thinking, *If he does kill me, I probably deserve it.* I thought about that promise over the years. As I went off to college and lived my life, I would stop every so often and wonder if my bullying had metastasized into a hidden hatred in him.

Years later, when I turned thirty-two, Luke didn't kill me. We had become friendly in adulthood and hadn't fought in years. He'd married a beautiful woman, bought a nice house, had a good job. He had friends and a pool and things looked good. I had just come home from living in South America for a year. I was two years older than Luke, and the only thing I owned was a laptop. I had a birthday party and Christmas with the family—my birthday falls right before Christmas—and, sure enough, he didn't murder me that day.

Throughout my thirty-second year, I wondered a few

times if it would come. It wasn't that I thought he was violent. It was that I thought I might deserve it.

I've had only one recurring dream in my life. It first came to me when I was in high school. In it, I am hiking with my brother through a forest. We are friends in the dream. He steps over a log, and just as I'm about to step behind him, I see a huge snake about to strike at him.

I push Luke out of the way, and as I do, the snake misses him and hits me square in the back. I feel its fangs enter me, feel the venom flow through my limbs. And while I writhe on the ground in pain, my brother stands over me, blank faced. "Luke, go get help!" I say. And he replies, disinterestedly, "Help yourself," before walking away.

They say you can't die in a dream. That you'll wake up just before you do. That is not true. Each time I've had this dream, I die. I feel my consciousness slip away, and then nothing.

I thought about that dream last year when I did a multiday therapy workshop outside of Nashville. It's called Onsite. They specialize in trauma and mental health. The workshop is hard to explain, but it's kind of like a retreat mixed with therapy and horses and incredible meals. I did it right before my first book came out. No phones. No booze or cigarettes or even exercise. Nothing you can use to escape how you feel. This is where I heard about the theory from the beginning of this section—about how your world at nine years old can define the person you become. The workshop is meant to help people get their inner lives in order so that they can thrive in their outer ones. It isn't woo-woo or new-age; it's science and psychology and summer camp. I did it with about twenty other people.

Onsite specializes in experiential therapy. It isn't simply talk therapy, which is what most of us think when we hear "therapy." In this program they do group experiences. You're in multihour sessions every day with the same group of people and two therapists guiding you. The main part of your work involves re-creating your childhoods using one another as metaphorical stand-ins. If it was my turn, for example, the therapist would ask me to create my family in the center of the room. Someone played my mom. Someone else played my dad. My sister. My stepdad. My brother. Then I would walk around the circle and explain the dynamic between each character. The therapist asked, "What did you need to hear from your mother?" She asked me to stand in my mother's place and say it. Then, the person playing my mother would step back into place and speak those words to me.

This can sound silly. But therapists have discovered that putting the conversation into space, giving it shape and size and movement, reaches more parts of the brain than we normally access. It isn't just talking and internal narrative. It's hearing words come from someone else. It's standing next to someone. It's hugging. Your brain doesn't think only in words. It thinks in feelings and spatial structures, too. It comprehends distance and tone. And most important: It grasps concepts through metaphor. The brain understands best when it can map reality into a simile. By replaying and reenacting an experience—having a conversation that you needed to hear but one that never happened—you reach deeper into your subconscious, into the frightened lizard brain, and from there, begin healing it.

This kind of work is used to uncover trauma or shame or

fear stored in the old core of the brain. This is the part of the brain that evolved before our consciousness to help us survive. To jump at a snake or gasp at a bear. If it doesn't do its job, all our pontificating about solar systems and critical race theory are worthless. Traumatic memories sit in that part of the brain forever . . . until we deal with them. Until we heal them through proper grieving.

In my final session of the workshop, after we'd laid the groundwork of my family's structure and dynamics, I was asked, "What is something you want to work on? What is a place of shame for you?" And I knew immediately what I wanted to do. It surprised me, because I hadn't thought about it in years. But it was an example of that moment when you know the thing you're afraid to say is exactly what you should say. I didn't want to pull it into the light because it would force me to look at a side of myself that I feared.

I told the therapist that I wanted to re-create my teenage years. To work on something that brought me shame and pain.

"What age?" she asked.

"Probably thirteen or fourteen years old."

"Okay, build your family as it was then.'

So I had people in the group play my mother, stepdad, and sister. And I asked my friend Danica to play my brother, Luke. The therapist then had me speak as my brother, telling me what he needed when we were teenagers and what his experience was.

I stepped in his shoes and spoke to me. "I only ever loved you. And you hated me. I was only ever nice to you. And you hated me. You gave me a stutter. You hurt me."

An enlightened defense leapt to mind as I stood there: *I hated you because you kept Mom's attention. You were cute and everyone thought you were so adorable. No one said anything to me. I was invisible because of you. I hated you because you took my mother away from me.*

His response came to me as well. *I had serious health problems. I didn't want to take attention from you. You were the smart one who got good grades and was a star everywhere we went. You wouldn't have died. I actually could have died.*

The simple act of having someone stand before me, holding space for my brother, speaking words I couldn't hear or didn't have the bravery to confront . . . it unlocked something. I pictured the ingredients of trauma—how, in my childlike insecurity and self-protectionism, I was likely a source of trauma for my brother. Building deep wounds in the foundation of who he is.

I began sobbing. My friend Danica stood in front of me, looking up with eyes bursting with empathy as I begged for forgiveness. I was facing the scary truth at my core, that perhaps I am mean and cruel. I, at my core, am rotten.

After that experience, Danica "de-rolled." She put her hands on my shoulders and said, "I am not your brother. I am Danica." This is a formality that helps the emotional brain disconnect the fire of what just happened from the person standing in that role. Everyone hugged me and encouraged me to write Luke a letter. To tell him that I was sorry. Even if I thought he was over it, clearly I wasn't. If only to heal me. And perhaps to heal him. Because in the end, it was him who received the cruelty. Yes, the perpetrator suffers the rot and often ends up spiritually worse. But that doesn't make them the victim.

I planned to write the letter. But I didn't. I left the workshop and slipped back into my life. I saw my brother at dinner at our mom's house and hugged him and complimented his shirt and freshly washed truck. I asked him how everything was. I was a bit over the top with the niceties. But I didn't write the letter. I was just a kid when I tormented Luke. He was a kid, and he had turned out wonderful and fine. No harm, no foul.

My masculine fear of sentimentality worked against me. It froze me.

Eight months later, we had a Sibling Dinner. This is a tradition my sister started where the four of us get together and drink wine and eat and read passages from books and have singing competitions and do accents and smoke cigarettes. No parents allowed. We're adults now and live in different parts of the country, and it's not easy to see one another. It's also hard to overcome that strange aversion to awkwardness that is so common in families. The effortless banter of friendship vanishes with family. We have trouble talking about anything serious or encouraging one another.

Sibling Dinner was my older sister's attempt to overcome that. Whenever I'm home from California, she cooks and invites us all over—me, my brother, and our younger sister—and sets conversation topics. At this most recent one, my sister asked a grenade of a question. After food and enough wine to loosen our tongues, she sat us around the patio table, lit up a cigarette, and asked, "What is one thing you most regret?"

My immediate response was to take the philosopher's position. *I don't really have regrets. Life is full of lessons and each one got me here. So, here I am. To remove any actions from the past would rob me of the growth today.*

But there was my little brother, sitting across from me. He had his hand on his lovely wife's knee. A thought poked up like a whack-a-mole in the center of my brain. *You regret how you treated Luke. You regret how cruel you were. Say it, you coward motherfucker.*

"I regret how I didn't try in school. I was so afraid of failure, I'd rather take B's than try for A's and fail," I said.

My siblings nodded and then took turns sharing. They said some sweet things. Nothing shocking. I felt relieved that the exercise had gone past me. And also pathetic for not taking this opportunity to say the right thing. To apologize. That lazy idiot teenager inside of me had taken the wheel.

Then it was Rebekah's turn. Only she didn't share a regret. She skipped right over herself and looked at me. "Okay, say something else. Let's do another round."

"But you didn't go!" I said.

"I'll go at the end. This is my house. Go again."

Shit. My mother's voice came to my mind. All the times she had encouraged me to write my brother a kind note. Or to call him. Or to tell him how impressed and proud I was of him. It all felt so contrived and silly. She even said once that I should "actively reconcile" with Luke. I remember saying, "Mom, what are you talking about? He has a great life now, and I'm off in California. He doesn't care about that stuff."

"I bet it would mean a lot to him," she said. Some small

thing inside me wondered if he had talked to her about it. If he had expressed adult hurt.

Another memory leapt to mind. For years, I would refer to my brother only as "Puke." It was a funny distortion of his name, taking the piss out of each other like brothers do. When he was twenty-five and I was twenty-seven, I called him Puke at some point over Christmas, and he snapped. "I'm twenty-five years old," he said. "You can't call me 'Puke' anymore. Please stop." I was stunned. I'd never heard him speak like that. Like a man. With boundaries. Embarrassed and immediately joking, gaslighting him probably, I said, "Oh, wow, okay. Didn't know it was such a big deal." But I never called him that again.

This all flashed in my brain in seconds. As if some bigger truth I'd been covering was sitting in the room, suddenly visible. Rebekah was staring at me, waiting for me to speak. I wondered if Mom had put her up to this.

"I guess, well, I do regret the way I treated Luke," I said. I was talking to Rebekah, not to Luke. Luke's wife, Anna, suddenly sat up, leaned in to listen to me, utterly absorbed. "I was so mean, and cruel, and he was only ever loving and nice to me. And that wasn't right.

"If I could do it all over again," I looked directly at Luke, "I'd be a good brother to you." Anna's eyes had tears in them. Which shook me.

Luke was looking at the ground. "That's all I needed to hear," he said.

Anna was rubbing her husband's leg. "I wondered if this would ever happen. I am so happy I could cry," she said, tears coming out of her smiling eyes.

A wave of hot shame poured from my cheeks. Shame at realizing how much pain my brother still carried. How he must've talked about this with Anna many times. How they'd lived with me, the villain in their story, all these years. And yet they still loved me. Now I'd finally said something, a shitty little apology, and it lifted a foot-thick blanket of ash that had covered us for two decades.

"Luke, I am so sorry. I love you. You are an amazing man, in spite of how shitty I treated you. I love you so much."

"That's all I needed to hear," he said. Glancing at me but mostly looking away. His head nodding at nothing. "That's all I needed to hear."

WHEN I COME home for the holidays, I stay at my mom's house. The house I grew up in.

She puts out her seasonal decorations and tidies my old room. She washes the dogs. She plans a family dinner. She walks me into the dining room to show me the place settings.

She wants to say, "I love you more than anything and I would do anything for you and I wish you would move back to Nashville and I'd love to see you every day and hear all that you're doing and be best friends and we should write together and plan some trips in the motor home and I'm getting older and time is precious and I'm so proud of you and I don't want anything to be unsaid."

But she knows if she said all of that, I would shut off. I would get quiet, freeze up, and make an excuse about having to go work at a coffee shop. I still have that teenage instinct to leave the nest when I am around her, to receive my mother's affection and attachment as fuel to leave. I can't help it. I hate that I can't help it.

She wants to watch me eat the breakfast she made me. She wants to say all the things in the world. But she can't. So she asks, "Do you have any laundry you need me to do?"

I want to say, "You are the best mom that has ever lived. You have made me who I am. You are clever and kind and true and generous and a living example of the type of person I want to be." But I don't say that. I say, "No, Mom, I'm all good."

"Well . . . okay," she says. She pauses, trying to think of some other way she can serve me. "Let me know when you do."

Mom, I know you'll read this. So this is me telling you. Putting it in print. In my cowardly, masculine, roundabout way.

I'M GOING TO paraphrase something I read somewhere. (Was it on Twitter? Tumblr? Instagram? Reddit? A group text? This is the trouble with too much information from too many sources coming from that little glowing screen in your hand.)

Imagine you're a parent, and your kid is always playing videogames in their room. You give them grief about it. You tell them they never socialize and that they are being rude and disrespectful. You have family over and finally the kid comes out to engage. You say, "Ooooh, look who it is! The old hermit makes a rare appearance! Thank you for gracing us with your presence!" Your voice drips with sarcasm. You make fun of your kid in front of the family. The kid feels like shit. Called out. If I was them, I'd go right back to my room.

Why do we punish people for finally doing the thing we wished they'd do? For making steps in the right direction?

When I spend time with family, I'm reminded of the ever-present ghost of the unsaid. The hardened hearts. The brothers who no longer speak, the life choices whispered and worried about in private. It is remarkable how hard it is for families to talk about things. To shine sunlight on the wounds in the basement.

I also see this in spouses. Tiny cuts accumulate into a tone of annoyance that colors their every conversation. It's the grown-up version of pinching your little brother in the backseat and telling Mom that nothing happened. "She won't even let me near a motorcycle!" "That's not what I said!" They litigate their conversations in front of you, trying to shame each other in front of an audience.

Contrast this with the way we treat our friends. We listen. We share our every thought. We take in new information and give our best. We light up with attention and care. We are hard to offend. Something in us wants to be chosen, not bought. A bird on a branch, not a rooted tree.

But when all goes to hell, those unbreakable bonds—those people tethered to you by history or covenant—they are often the ones who save your life. Who provide a ground zero. They are home.

I wonder what it takes to give our bright-shining best to those we're bound to. To treat our family like friends. To overpower the instinct to retract and avoid. I don't know. I seem to enjoy sealing myself, closing myself off from showing that kindness. I keep doing it. The head has trouble over-riding whatever wiring makes me want to run.

I'M GRATEFUL TO my parents for instilling in me the desire to open doors. To follow the creek upstream, to turn down windy roads that take too long, to turn over rocks and look for snakes, to value wisdom and experience over the conventions of our assembly-line society.

I was terribly strange as a child. I was obsessed with dinosaurs, daytime talk shows, and writing moody songs on the piano in the dark. I would dip G.I. Joes in nail polish remover and light them on fire in the backyard. My poor parents. Yet they never asked me to be anything but myself. In sixth grade my mom lied to the school office and told them I had a doctor's appointment. She picked me up at lunch and took me to see the rerelease of *Star Wars* on opening day. I thought heaven had come to earth.

GROWING UP, I realized I was immune to poison ivy. I think I knew my little brother was not. I went up to him and said, "Hey, look what I can do," and rubbed the poison leaves all over my face. "I can do that, too!" he said, as any younger brother would. And he rubbed and rubbed.

He had to go to the hospital because his face swelled up like a red beanbag. His eyes sealed shut. I got in big trouble.

One time I was sitting in my room drawing dinosaurs when my sister knocked on my door. I opened the door and there she was, with her evil best friend, DD. They had an aerosol can and a lighter. Before I could react, they blew a giant ball of fire in my face. I screamed. I hit a Mariah Carey note. I was so furious, I shouted "BURN IN HELL!" to them. It's the only time I've ever really cursed someone.

In retaliation, I snuck into my sister's room that night and unplugged everything. I unscrewed the lightbulbs. Then I called the house phone, knowing she'd pick up in her room. I disguised my voice to sound like a stranger. I said I was stalking her and had turned off the power in the house. She tried to turn her lamp on. It didn't work. She screamed bloody murder and locked herself in the bathroom for an hour. This is my confession, Rebekah. That was me.

Kids do strange things. Bad things. We test to see the consequences of our actions. We peacock and make power plays. We see what we can get away with.

Adults do the same thing, I think. The testing is just more complex, more hurtful, harder to understand. Adultery. Avoidance. Secret lives. Midlife crises.

Growing up often looks like covering up.

Do you remember that phase before middle school, before life revealed to you yourself and your body and the differences of others? When you were a creature of pure curiosity? When you still told your parents you loved them, and you were too pure to see in their faces that they knew you'd stop saying it soon? When your dad still picked you up? (Do you remember the last time one of your parents picked you up and held you? There was a last time, and no one noticed.) Remember when the creek at the bottom of the hill was all the adventure in the world? When you loved what you loved and gave two shits if anyone else did? For me, it was dinosaurs and comics and snakes and creatures in the creek.

Remember those few years of utter clarity. When you were smart enough for language but young enough for wonder. Where love was love and comparison was a foreign idea.

My life seems to be a pendulum-like journey, searching for that feeling and grabbing it as I swing past, crumpling it up like a T-shirt that smells nice and pushing it into my face.

I REMEMBER MY dad saying, "This guy I know didn't want to raise his kids out here in Spring Hill. He thought it was too rural. But I told him how my kids grew up out here, and how the country made them imaginative. How my son Jed's favorite thing was going to the dump."

"Oh my gosh, I forgot," I said. "My favorite days were when we'd go to the dump and I'd find stuff!"

We were too remote to have trash service. Every week or two, my dad would fill the bed of his truck with trash and broken tools, and we'd head out to the Maury County dump. He'd let me ride in the back sometimes with all the junk. When we pulled up, there would be giant metal containers with garbage divided by category. Plastic, metal, paper. Inside these containers were discarded toys, magazines, treadmills, shiny metal things. I'd poke around with my dad calling from another container. "Be careful now. Don't touch things that look sharp."

I always found something. An old man's cane. A perfectly good G.I. Joe. A spark plug that could work as an alien cannon for my Ninja Turtles. I couldn't believe people would throw away such good stuff. But I was so glad they did.

We'd finish up and head back to the farm. Maybe stop on the way and get a Dr Pepper. Dad would play Sting on the truck's cassette player. And I'd feel rich with my new things.

I saw *I, Tonya* last year, the movie about the ice skater Tonya Harding. I remember being a kid when the news showed Nancy Kerrigan crying about her knee, and Tonya Harding was turned into a villain on skates. I've spent my entire life making Tonya Harding jokes. The movie is funny and strange and silly, but it also portrays another side of Harding. A girl raised without love. A girl mocked from the beginning. A girl who thought skating might be her ticket out of all that mess. And when things got hard, she made some pretty massive mistakes. The frightened girl, stunted by fear and self-defense, made choices like a frightened child. Maybe she's a heartless monster, an opportunist, a creep. Maybe she is beyond redemption. Maybe she's not.

I think about poor kids who sell drugs or drop out of school. What if the only thing modeled for them was distrust? What if leaving the neighborhood was a form of betrayal? I am astonished that anyone overcomes their past.

There is a saying—I will screw it up, but it goes something like, "If we could comprehend all, we would understand all;

if we understood all, we would forgive all." I think it's more complicated than that. Even when we understand someone, their actions may still cause incredible harm, and the harm must be stopped. But it's also true that the method of stopping matters. Hatred, mockery, and caricature seem to embolden the wounded who continue to wound.

How do people overcome? I doubt many people become better after being hated. Pride latches on to old positions, raises its voice, fights to the death. But I've seen kindness and understanding soften the fortress walls.

When has mockery saved a soul? When has a shouting match ended in mutual elevation? When to be gentle, and when to revolt? What is the way to lasting peace?

LET ME PAINT a picture: If your mom worked hard and planted many crops, and no calamities came to ruin her farm, you would grow up with a full belly. But if your mom had a farm and didn't work hard, or if a tornado or thief came and took everything, you would grow up hungry. Your mom would be ashamed, or broken. In her brokenness, maybe she would hate you and herself.

Either way, we don't earn our beginnings. You didn't earn a successful mother any more than another child earned an unsuccessful one.

You, the well-fed child, would be strong and have enough leisure time to develop important skills, ones that would make you competitive. You would assume your childhood is what all other childhoods are like. You may meet the child of an unsuccessful mom on the playground and ask why their clothes are dirty. They would be ashamed.

Now imagine this cycle being repeated over ten generations.

There is a paradox in our thinking: to believe that the efforts or misfortunes of our parents greatly determine our lives, while simultaneously believing that we come into life on equal footing, and that our successes are ours to boast about.

This dynamic seems responsible for the existential tension currently in the air, in our politics and in the big societal problems that we can't seem to solve. We wake up into life profiting from, or disadvantaged by, the events of our ancestors. We're proud of some of the things, and we ignore others. Some of us stand on the shoulders of devils, slaveholders, and crooks, profiting now, and do not even know.

And yet here we are, responsible for our own lives, taking credit for our hard work and careers, blaming the junkie for his weakness, praising the entrepreneur for her work ethic. Ignoring the puppeteers of history and consequence.

I JOKE THAT God sometimes gets busy and doesn't have time to make each person unique. So he hits Ctrl-C and makes copies. There are a few members of my family who seem this way. My aunt Lee Lee, my aunt Abby, and me. We are soul copies. We prank-call together. We put flowers down our shirts. We collapse the passing years with one loud cackle and clasping fingers at a joke. We are glad God was hurried.

. . .

"I DON'T BELIEVE in having children," a friend of mine said. "I think it's wrong to bring a child into this world."

"What? Why?" I said.

"If I could choose to not have been born, I would choose that. It's not worth it. Too much pain. Too much suffering. It feels like an injustice."

That sent me for a spin. I love being alive. I testify to this every day. I find beauty in garbage and laughter in traffic. I wake up in love. Many people don't feel this way.

When I wrote my first book, I thought about this a lot. About how my words would be misinterpreted. About how people who see the world differently from me might hate it. Find it annoying, sentimental, and false. How I'd be accused of this motive or that. Of being out of touch or privileged and blinded by it.

I truly don't know what to do with the diversity of experiences in this life, except to offer kindness and speak when I can, and listen when I should.

One of my mentors often says, "I don't judge others, tell people that they're wrong or I'm right. The truth works itself out. Life is an orchestra. I'm here to play my note. No one else's. And it's not my job to tell them how to play. I listen to their music. And maybe they listen to mine. I just want to make the music I'm supposed to make."

WHAT IS EXPECTED of us when we disagree?

What happens when you believe government should help, and your brother thinks it should get out of the way? What happens when you believe God puts a human soul in a fertilized egg, and your sister doesn't believe in souls and believes that a fetus is part of a woman's body until it can live on its own? What happens when you believe you were born a woman in a man's body—you believe it so deeply that you're willing to endure public ridicule and shame to be your true self—and your father thinks you're mentally ill?

We know what usually happens. Relationships collapse. Family members become strangers to one another. Or enemies. The other is mocked, demonized, or prayed for.

There's a place in Los Angeles called the Museum of Tolerance, and I always thought its name was so unfortunate. Tolerance? That's the best we can hope for? Why not the Museum of Acceptance? of Love? of Respect? As I've gotten older, though, I've seen how worldviews are not as malleable as I once thought. An argument is as effective as a light breeze. It can tip you over, but only if you're teetering or loose. Childhood and biology are the top influencers. Second to them: experience and relationship.

Tolerance is not the same as acceptance. I don't want to accept a belief I think is wrong, or hurtful, or dangerous. That would betray my morals. But I believe in the dignity of human agency and the complexity of experience. I think we can have grace for one another and the strength to stand up for ourselves. That's tolerance. Sometimes that's the best we can do.

That, and the long, slow work of truth. "Truth is a stubborn thing." It corrects, it rebukes, but most of all, it takes its time. Foolishness can spend centuries riding on the back of half-truth.

How do we stay in relationship with one another? I've seen humor go a long way. Goodwill. The belief that people are trying their best, doing what they think is right.

Start there. Seek understanding. It is much harder to hate a friend.

Home

I remember peeing in the trash can in my bedroom when I was four years old. There wasn't a why. I just wanted to. The bathroom was five feet down the hall.

Another time, I woke up puking in that same bedroom. I was under the covers late that night when the chaos in my stomach jolted me awake. Puke was all over my pillow, pouring out of my mouth as my consciousness came online. It frightened me. I walked through the dark hall, my stomach still convulsing. Crying. Not loudly. Just confused little sobs. I woke up my mom and led her to the scene.

I have other memories in that house, but I'm almost certain they come from photographs. There was a hallway on the first floor with an old church pew against the wall. The front door was connected to the driveway by a brick path. I have animated those pictures in my head and claimed to remember them.

We lived in a big white house on a farm in middle Tennessee. The land rolled and piled itself up like the covers of an unmade bed. No big hills, but sloping changes in elevation everywhere you looked. If you walked across the big field in front of the house and through some clumps of trees, you would find the creek. I was allowed to go there alone from a very young age. To explore without supervision. I would walk in the creek and look for turtles, fruitlessly grab at fish. Stare at the universe of tadpoles and minnows living in their little water world.

My parents divorced when I was five or six. I don't know the precise date, and I've never asked. My mom got custody and kept the big white house. My dad bought the farm next door and moved in with his new wife. My mom, finding this arrangement to be perverted, moved us up to Nashville, thirty miles away.

I didn't get angry, question why my parents weren't together, or think about what it meant that we were leaving the farm for a little blue house in the suburbs. I was too young to know that divorce wasn't the natural way of things. I just lived as if it were all inevitable. Maybe I cried. Maybe I complained. I don't have memory of it.

As my mom adjusted to the trauma of her broken marriage, we moved between a few rented houses. The blue one. Then a white one. Then Mom bought a brick house in a nice suburb south of Nashville, a decent house whose backyard linked to a forested park. We moved into that house when I was eight, around that fateful age where the self becomes a thing. My real memories start there. That brick house, where my mom still lives thirty years later, is home to me. So is the farm before it. The little blue house after the farm is not. Neither is the white ranch house after it. It probably has to do with time spent. I had numerous years in the farmhouse. And my entire adolescence in the brick house. Ask me today, and I will say Nashville is my home. That I lived on a farm when I was little, and that's why I feel at home in nature.

As a kid, I didn't have some articulated sense of what home was. I just knew I had food when I was hungry and parents who loved me and siblings whom I wanted to fight. Visiting my dad down on the farm kept me connected to that land. I grew up in that creek. Until college, I would make time to wade in that water whenever I was there.

The idea of home begins to crystallize once you're old enough to see your childhood from a distance. Maybe it's in high school. Certainly college. When you've got a fully working brain, you can recall fuzzy, borderless impressions from your younger mind, and the locations where they were formed—memories that coalesced into important ones, the things that shaped your budding identity. Home, for the child, is discovered after the fact.

WHETHER HOME WAS tumultuous or idyllic, transient or stationary, we all form some sense of where we are from. Even if you hated where you grew up, you hated it with the energy of knowing there were places you could have loved. We long for a sense of being from somewhere. A land. A culture. A family. This is, of course, a desire to belong—not just to a group, but to the world. We want to feel like we inevitably sprung up from the soil. And disconnection from this feeling turns us cold and mean, sad or twisted, into conquerors or wanderers or consumers. A soul disconnected from place has no reason to care, beyond wanting what it can take from that place in order to survive. No real knowledge of the interconnectedness of ecosystems, of economies, of people and needs. Uncoupled from the world, we become its destroyers.

I've always wanted to own land. I will see a farm, a rolling hill, or an oak tree with a swing, and I will ache to have it in the way I ache for the love of a man. I've seen beach houses on a cliff that hurt my heart. It feels like my spirit is having some kind of spatial emergency. It can no longer live in my rib cage. It must explode out and absorb or unite with whatever it wants.

Ancient humans didn't own land. That idea of ownership didn't spread until we started living in agricultural societies. But our ancestors didn't have to. There was no such thing as "nature" and "man-made." It was all one thing. This is why so many traditional cultures worshipped mountains and rivers, gave them sacred status. They sensed that those things played some part in creating them. They were family. The most integrated sense of belonging that exists.

In our crowded cities and societies, we want this, to feel the land. I think that is why New Yorkers talk about New York so much. How it's alive and never sleeps and flows and has an energy. They make it a thing that they belong to, belong *in*. They give it a spirit and talk to it like a god.

THE FARMHOUSE WHERE I grew up has been converted into a restaurant called Mockingbird. You can eat dinner in the room where I learned to walk. There is a bar where the kitchen used to be. You can get a cocktail in the spot where I peeked over the counter to watch my grandmother make doughnuts from scratch.

Most of the surrounding farm was sold to a hospital. My dad still has some land on the other side of our old house. There is now a wide paved road that cuts straight through the middle of the farm. It passes over the site of a little stream where I once found a jar buried in mud and convinced myself it had come from ancient Greece. I must've been seven or eight. I brought it to my dad, buzzing from my archeological find. "This must be worth something! How old do you think it is?" I asked.

I'm sure he could tell it was simply a little soap jar. But it was beautiful, cream colored, and it did look a bit old. He encouraged my little Indiana Jones moment. "We should go down to the pawnshop and see what they'll give for it," he said. "I bet it's worth some money."

Wow. I felt lucky. The fruits of being a curious explorer. The finder of El Dorado.

My dad drove as I rode in the bed of the truck, cradling my treasure.

The rusty guy at the pawnshop looked at the jar. "Wow, this is beautiful." I bet my dad was standing above me, making eyes at the guy. He seemed to labor over what to say. I was certain he was doing some complex calculation of its value. Then he spoke. "I don't think it's rare. I can give you two dollars."

I was crestfallen. I looked at my jar, its delicacy and shine immediately transformed into junk. I collected myself as best a seven-year-old could, and tried to play it off. "I thought so," I lied, and stared at the floor. I felt betrayed by my dad. By the jar itself. I bargained internally. Maybe this pawnshop guy didn't know what he was talking about. Maybe I needed a second opinion.

"No thanks, I'll keep it," I said. "Maybe its value will go up." I had heard of the stock market, after all. I took the jar home, and it sat on my dresser for a decade, looking at me blankly. I never did anything with it, but it always held this touch of possibility, of secret value.

That jar is gone now. So is the creek where I found it. A few years ago, the town filled it with sand and gravel, then paved it over. It's under a busy road.

One afternoon, my mom and I went down and did a walk-through of the new restaurant. It was beautiful. I felt my little self running over the hardwood floors, curiously watching people eat, listening to their stories, wondering if they wonder about me.

When we left, driving out over that new road, we passed two teenage boys holding skateboards. They were walking on a sidewalk built on top of my childhood. They know nothing about that. They live in the brand-new neighborhood at the end of this new road. They are kissing girls and headed down to the big creek. School's out and it's summer. This is their childhood now.

LANDSCAPE HAS SUCH an effect on me. The stone cliffs and dark forests of Vermont create a privacy in me, a tender darkness. Some glowing internal space that I cradle. In fall, the coming cold of December asks for my respect. These winters have made Vermonters hard workers. A tight community. Land worshippers. The place carves personalities into the people who live there.

When I'm in Los Angeles, the sunshine and the dusty afternoon light give me energy and optimism. Maybe that's why the city is a churning wash of hope.

The heat of the South, of my native Tennessee, is a polarizing thing. It can turn you soft and charming, or angry and isolated. You want sweet tea or booze. The southern drawl, the cotton fields, the kindness and the cruelty, have these hot humid summers as their setting.

Travel helps me know all of my selves. In Vermont I am a farmer, a forest wanderer, a small-town guy. Even Burlington feels too big. In New York I am a culture glutton, a café philosopher, a socialite. In Los Angeles I am a weekend warrior, a camper, and a Hollywood coattails rider. I am both the Wild West and the Internet.

Each city and state introduces me to some hidden part of myself.

I GOOGLED "WHY do leaves change color in the fall?" and expected there to be some important evolutionary purpose in the answer. Maybe animals need to see the color for some reason. Maybe the trees process the last bit of summer's sun through shades of yellow and red. No. It's because the green chlorophyll dies away, and what's left are the other pigments. Meaning, the beauty serves no purpose. Somehow, that makes it all the more beautiful to me.

. . .

I LOVE ASKING people "What is the place you're always trying to get back to?" Is it a beach somewhere? Or childhood
summer camp? Or with your ex before it got complicated
and sad? Or a camping trip with your best kindred friends?
Where do you run back to?

IMAGINE YOU LIVE on a small farm. Big enough to have all
that you need. Water. Cows. Chickens. Vegetables. A barn to
store things for winter. Plenty of trees for nuts and some
firewood. That little bit of land is all you needed to keep you
and your family alive.

Most likely you would take care of your land. You
wouldn't cut down so many trees for firewood that you destroy the forest. You wouldn't let your sewage leak into the
pond, because you drink from that pond. You wouldn't
breed so many cows that it would crush the chickens. You
wouldn't feed the chickens chemicals that could hurt your
kids. You see what I'm getting at. In order to have the things
you need to live well and be healthy, your space needs to be
kept in balance. A little bit of this, a little bit of that. Give
and take.

One family can comprehend one farm. You have the
bandwidth to worry about the birth of a calf on Monday
and a fox in the henhouse on Tuesday. You can see your own
forest, and eyeball how many trees you can cut for winter
firewood.

Now zoom out to your current, real life. How many
trees are in your hometown? A thousand? Maybe a million? How many cows would you drive past if you went

on a road trip from California to Maine? A bunch. How many rivers are there? My God, who knows. So, if you had some pee in a bottle, would you dump it in a random river? Yeah, why not. The water dilutes it, so who cares. The burger you ate yesterday—where did the meat come from? No idea. Where did the wheat grow that made the bun? Where did the chicken lay the egg for the scramble?

Absolutely no clue.

The more people there are, the more we can cooperate and specialize. If you lived on a farm, you would spend much of your day, maybe all of it, milking cows and repairing chicken coops and weeding the garden and patching the roof on the barn. You would have little time for poetry. For inventing. For music or games. You'd come in at dark, exhausted. Only when we specialize can you find some free time. Now it's your neighbor's job to milk too many cows, so that she has extra, and you can buy it from her. Maybe with your free time, you write a song that the other farmers love. And they pay you to sing it to them.

Now it is no longer your job to know where the cows are and how they are doing. It's your job to write songs. You don't watch the chickens lay their eggs. You buy them. You're too busy to worry about the forest over the hill.

Expand this a few billion times, and it's no wonder that we abuse natural things, the poisoning of rivers and overfishing of the oceans. I have no idea how many tuna are in the sea. Should I? I'm busy writing songs, and my fridge is full.

. . .

I WAS IN upstate Wisconsin a few summers ago, way out in the forest at a friend's cabin. One day, while wandering away to pee, I saw a little flower on the edge of a meadow. It was violet and blue, some glowing mixture of the two. It looked like the kind of flower that a tiny fairy would wear as a hat. It was delicate and feminine and meticulously formed. Symmetrical and crisp. And it was hidden in a mess of weeds and tall grass, with no trail in sight.

I am, without a doubt, the only human who ever saw or will ever see that flower. It fought so hard to survive and grow and live. I saw it there, and I loved it. Only me. I guess I would've loved it even if I had never seen it, because the thing in me that loved the flower was already there, waiting to witness it from my spot in the weeds.

WE SPENT THE vast majority of our time as *Homo sapiens* living in small groups. Usually 150 people or smaller. We looked like our fellow tribe members. Our skin color was mostly the same. Our language the same. Our culture clear and regimented through the authority of elders, superstition, and oral tradition. The tribe that lived on the other side of the mountain was alien and probably dangerous. Perhaps we traded seashells with them. Perhaps we warred with them. We certainly didn't understand them.

Then, ten or twelve thousand years ago, we discovered agriculture, and therefore, dependable food. With a secure food source, we quit migrating. We built walls and defended our grain. We organized into groups much larger than our families, where we no longer knew everyone's name. How did we get along? If we couldn't trust our neighbor because of blood, we trusted her because the two of us worshipped the same god, the same king, the same spirits. You're the same religion as me, so you are with me. With dependable food and this myth-driven trust, our villages became towns, our towns cities, and our cities nations. We broke our giant tribes into classes. We created ruling elites. We deified them to give them authority. Structural inequality was born. We could no longer feel the impact of some of our sins on the larger group, on strangers, so we codified morality into religion. If your neighbor didn't see you steal, the all-seeing God did.

We are feeling animals first, thinking apes second. We make decisions based on how we feel much more than what logic and data tell us. We can feel the sadness on the face of a starving family member. We feel it less when a spreadsheet tells us more children die of dysentery than terrorist attacks. We aren't wired to make urgent decisions about numbers. We respond to faces, to problems in close proximity to us. Of course it's this way. We didn't evolve for a million years worrying about the fate of families on the other side of the world.

Problems that are too complex to comprehend, or grasp with immediacy, have a name: hyperobjects. The global economy is a hyperobject. When I buy a cheap T-shirt, I can be warned that its price reflects an enormous scaffolding of oppression, land abuse, worker abuse, and toxic chemicals. But our brains want cheap things that look nice. This shirt will make me look good in front of my community. I can feel that. I can't feel a supply chain that stretches across the globe to places I've never even heard of. Even if I logically know it.

Our impact on the natural world is a hyperobject. Perhaps the most pressing one to ever face our species. We know this intellectually. All the experts agree. But we have a lot of trouble feeling it. And therefore, change is happening as a trickle. Those wired to feel hyperobjects a bit more, react more. Those wired to ignore them (most of us), do less. We know that if we do not learn to address these hyperobjects, we will greatly suffer. Perhaps collapse. We know this intellectually. But we simply cannot feel it, because so many of us are loving our comfortable lives.

And yet things change. A few hundred years ago, we all somehow agreed that colorful paper would become money and therefore powerful. Before that, we got millions, then billions of people to believe in a book of Jewish words and laws. More recently, millions of strangers started calling themselves "Americans" and feeling some level of fictional kinship.

In the same way, we must expand the myth of our role in the ecosystem of this planet. We are not separate from it. There is no "nature" and "civilization." There is only nature. And nature does not much care if we exist or not.

WHEN I WAS in second grade, my teacher asked the class to present your "big idea" in front of everyone. The assignment was to think of some good idea that would change the world for the better. It could be anything.

I knew immediately what I must do. I went home, got a poster board, and drew a horrible map of the United States. Then I drew vertical stripes down it, fat ones. Probably ten stripes. I colored in every other one to make America look like a candy cane.

The next day, as students talked about eternal recess or installing free candy dispensers in each desk, I got up and made my case.

"The world is overpopulated. I believe people should be allowed to live in only half of America, and the other half is for animals. I have made a map. People can live only in the dark stripes and animals only in the white ones. Buffaloes and wolves and other animals big and small. The stripes are up and down because animals need to migrate with the seasons. People can visit the animal stripes, but can't live there. People should also stop having so many babies. Thank you."

Why was I so concerned with overpopulation as a second grader? Why did I want to put the national parks system on steroids? I must've come into this world with certain cares and concerns. I know a lot of young parents now. If they have more than one kid, the universal revelation on the second child is, "They just show up with a personality. There's only so much that parenting does. This kid was the way he is from day one."

For some of us, it's like we're all born with a mysterious mission, something that bugs us from day one. Mine has been a love for the natural world.

I READ THAT the Swiss village of Lauterbrunnen is located in "the most spectacular glacial valley in the world." I went there last summer and wow, it is no hyperbole. It earned its title. As if God took a gelato scooper and drug it through the highest mountains. The Swiss have taken the imposing might of a mountain range and tamed it. Giving you cuddly cottages and churches perched on vertical cliffs and fields of cattle with bells around their necks. It fries your visual circuits. The cliff walls are made for giants. And then cascading waterfalls are everywhere. The creeks in the forests above suddenly leap from the edge and fall in slow motion. Some falling from such heights that they blow into mist before hitting the ground.

I always feel a certain sadness in seeing the "best" in the world. As if the journey is now over. The Internet or the travel book told me that this was the tallest, or the biggest, or the most spectacular, and now I've seen it.

There's a line in the movie *Away from Her* that goes something like, "There ought to be a place in the world that you always wanted to see, but never do see." I think about that often. Keeping some beauty beyond reach. So much of living is in the wanting, the reaching. I've never loved food more than during a long hunger. And after gorging myself in a moment's rapture, I swear to never eat again.

It is so common to want to see the best. If you're going to go to all the trouble to travel and see something, might as well see the biggest or the most impressive one, right?

I don't think so. Because anyone who has been in love knows that the alchemy of love springs from more than beauty alone. It is a busy cauldron of things.

I love the Alps, but I am a visitor there. The Rockies,

those are my mountains. I have memories there. Road-tripping to Lake City, Colorado, with my mom as a kid. Snowboarding in Utah in my twenties. Twelve years of going to a documentary film festival in Telluride. Telluride is my love, not because it is better or the best, but because it holds more than a decade of my fondest memories. It is made sacred to me by nostalgia, nature (of course), and tradition—forces that can turn the most modest valley in Missouri into heaven on earth. Telluride is spectacular, don't get me wrong. It is as close to Switzerland as the United States gets. But it is, by some measure, less extreme.

It is when our lives are put into places, spirit sewed to soil, that superlatives and lists of the "world's best" lose their power.

You decide what places have magic or not. Whether this cairn is a pile of rocks or a holy temple.

Isn't it strange that we find mountains beautiful? Evolutionarily, they would have represented a boundary, a block, a wall. A cold place of death. Right? Or take the Grand Canyon. It is dry and harsh, a nearly impenetrable impediment to our instinct to explore and master the land. But when we see it, we are moved. People worshipped it for centuries, and still do. But why? What business do we have finding this world and its magnitude beautiful? What benefit does it give us in our race for survival? Wouldn't a hungry antagonism better suit our animal brains?

Two hundred years ago, we did see the wilderness as a

foe, as an inexhaustible force. Even then, poetry was full of a love for nature, for the ocean, for the wild. Even now, when we see recent photos of deep space, of supernovas and clouds of colorful gas too large to understand—things no one in our genetic ancestry has ever seen—we see them for the first time and exclaim their beauty. Why? Why don't we fear?

Maybe an anthropologist knows, or an evolutionary biologist can tell me some theories. . . . I'd love to know. But not knowing is also fine. I enjoy feeling small before these spectacles of indifferent grandeur. I love slamming on the brakes to help a turtle cross the road. I love living in the belief that I belong, that we all do. I enjoy the feeling of loving something, and not knowing why.

THE WORLD IS perfectly sized. Too big to explore it all, but small enough to try.

ONE OF THE best gifts of travel is a reawakening of the sense of gratitude. For your own bed. For toilets. For traditions. For proximity to old friends.

In 2009, four years before biking from Oregon to Patagonia, I gave my bed away and decided to sleep on the floor. My room was an attic, and I slept on an IKEA rug with tons of blankets. I wanted to train my body to sleep well anywhere. It worked. But after living on a bicycle and sleeping for sixteen months in hammocks, in tents, on foam mattresses in people's garages, and in rickety bunks in rickety hostels, the idea of having a bed seemed like heaven in my mind. And when I got back to Los Angeles, to dinner with friends and documentary nights and beers in the back-yard, . . . I slid under the covers every night and read myself to sleep and couldn't believe any king anywhere ever had it better than I did.

This is the awakening that turns the poison of entitle-ment into a banquet of thanks. Travel is a splash of water in the face: "Wake up and look around. You have everything you need. Notice."

I'VE LEARNED THAT food is a word with a thousand mean-ings. That a bed can range from a cloud to a handful of wooden slats. That a handshake in one place is a double kiss in another. That the sound of a jackhammer in one city is a gunshot somewhere else. I grew up in a neigh-borhood with no fences, no broken glass lining the top of walls. The separation between properties was an invis-ible line between slopes of grass and trees. It never dawned on me how unusual that was for most of the world. In Argentina they are disgusted that Americans don't use bi-dets. In Brazil, they can't believe we don't take our tooth-brushes to work so we can brush after lunch. My Ugandan friend once refused to eat a chicken nugget. I asked, "Why?" She said "Gross! In Uganda, I raise my chickens next to my home and I know how they are. This place, I have no idea who has touched that chicken, or who killed it, prepared it. It's disgusting. How do I even know it is chicken?"

. . .

ALL LANDSCAPES ARE beautiful. The grasslands, the flat, wide prairies, the gentle hills—they all have their own charm. But when you see Yosemite, or Zion, or the Grand Canyon, something happens to you. These miracles of tectonics leave the eyes at a loss. Glancing up and down, we gasp. We laugh for no reason but disbelief. We slap the shoulders of our friends and say, "Can you believe it?"

The same grandeur can happen in the forming of a human soul. All spirits are beautiful, and worthy, and important. But some rare few are treasures of this planet, the best it has to offer. To be marveled at and made into holy sites.

THERE IS A reason we hike to the tops of mountains and climb to the tops of trees. A reason why we drool at skyscrapers and ride the gondola to the top. We want to see. Why? Because something in us wants to know the shape and body of the land from above. It answers a question being asked all the time just behind our minds. Maybe it was millions of years of wanting to know who or what was coming for us. Maybe it cheaply fulfills the dream of flight, a strange dream, almost a memory, implanted in us all from a past we never had. So far as we know.

. . .

ONE OF MY favorite feelings is something I call "second-hand rediscovery." It happens when you show someone the things and places you love, but for them it's the first time. You may have seen the place a million times, yet when you go there with a friend, you see it through their eyes and discover it for yourself all over again. In fact, you almost discover it better. In the sparkling eyes of your friend, you live both the astonishment of something new and the intimacy of something known, all at once.

In 2010, the nonprofit where I worked invited many of our Ugandan employees to San Diego to go on a speaking tour. They were all from northern Uganda, an area that was rural and, at the time, economically depressed. Most of them had never traveled at all. The majority were in their teens and twenties, young college kids excited to see a different side of the world. Uganda is a landlocked country, so one of the first things we did was take them to the beach.

One person in the group was older. His name was Norman. He was seventy-two years old, the father of our country director, and he wanted to travel and see America. He had a booming deep voice, skin as dark as obsidian, a long neck, and regal wrinkles. When we got to the beach, Norman walked out onto the sand and stopped, staring. He said, "This truly is a miracle. I thought I would live my whole life and only read of such a place." And he walked possessed, fully clothed, into the waves.

That day, I saw the ocean for the first time again.

. . .

WE FORGET THAT here in the present, we are the distant future to millions and the distant past to millions more. The Aztecs and the Egyptians could not have imagined that we would be walking through their temples with iPhones and sunglasses. We cannot fathom that in a few thousand years, some archeologist may find a flash drive full of photos from New York Fashion Week and assume that humans wore capes and angel wings and were surprisingly tall. When I visit Manhattan, I look at the buildings and pretend to be from the future, suddenly aware of how funny and beautiful every thing is.

I HAVE NOSTALGIA for the long, boring road trips my mom took me on as a kid. We couldn't afford hotels or flights, so we drove to parks and camped. Those drives were endless, and I thought the backseat of the station wagon was my prison. Now, years later, I dream of that backseat view of America, and I live the way I do, traveling constantly and writing about it.

I can have nostalgia for almost anything. That's how it works. It makes the events of your past integral in your present, as I'm sure they are. Nostalgia is how God sees all the time.

A MOUNTAIN, AS far as we can tell, doesn't know it exists. It is asleep forever. These temples of worship, giants of the earth, are sacred to almost every person who lives in their shadow. Songs have been written about them and to them. Prayers offered. Sacrifices left on their shoulders. And they sit, silent and dumb. Unaware that they exist at all.

We, with our parking tickets and college debt and misinterpreted texts and depressions and moments of nihilism and roller coasters and music festivals and heartbreaks—we are awake. Because of you, the universe is aware and observing itself. No matter how small and random you may feel, how meaningless, your ability to say, "That is beautiful," is a power that no mountain, no planet, no sun can imagine.

THE RAIN HAS been good to Tennessee. The corn is higher than a man on horseback. Whenever I see wild food, fruit trees that you can eat straightaway, berry bushes or carrots in the garden, I experience a sort of shock. "Wait, I can just eat this directly from the ground?"

What does it mean that it shocks me that real food would come from the earth, and not a supermarket? I was raised in the suburbs, where my closest connection to nature was turning over a log to find a snake or an earthworm. I see it as something other than me. I cannot believe that I am an animal, just like all of the earth's inhabitants. But with every rainstorm, the green leaf pushes up from the cracks in the pavement to say without judgment, "I am still here and have everything to teach you. Because unlike you, I am patient and know what I am."

. . .

IMAGINE IF WE could live a thousand years, and watch the world change like an advancing glacier. We would see the tribes and many nations of the United States be replaced by the mysterious white men from the eastern seas. We would be moved by these foreigners' ideas and virtues, and confounded by their selective blindness. We would see the ships arriving with hundreds of thousands of slaves, hunted and captured from the western coasts of Africa. We would see them fight and die for their freedoms, and white men in pulpits cry out to God to keep the holy institution of slavery alive. We would see young children used as labor in factories. We would see women sent to prison just for asking to vote. We would see interracial marriage become legal only forty years ago, in the face of wild protest at its unnatural sin. We would see a swell of conscience infect the world, slowly at first, and then spreading like a friendly virus.

And we, the tired and thawing ice, would see marriage reach the lives of all Americans in the year 2015. We, the old glacier, would scarcely believe that the humans of today could be the descendants of our dead friends of what felt like only yesterday. And our dream of becoming warm and welcoming water would feel closer than before. The thaw continues.

I LOVE BEING addicted to coffee. I tried giving it up once, because I didn't like the hold it had over me. I thought I could scare myself straight by reading about its health dangers online. But when I googled it, I found article after article about how good coffee is for you, and how the more you drink the better. More than five cups a day? Great for your heart! So that settled that.

I love the ritual of making it. The ritual of going to get it at a shop I visit so often that the baristas know my name. I love sludgy cowboy coffee, sipped around a morning campfire. Or even instant coffee put in boiling water. The way you wake up in the air chilled by the night, and, for once, your life has a clear and unconfused direction: Make coffee.

If only life was always as clean and uncluttered as it is in those first few moments of waking.

WHEN I IMAGINE where I want to live, the first thing that comes to mind is where I want to have that coffee in the morning. I picture the breakfast nook or the chair and the book and the coffee and the view. My second dream is where I will have a beer. I see afternoon light getting low and angled, sending yellow rays through the tree branches. Maybe on a back patio, or on a grassy bluff over the Pacific Ocean.

The imagined locations of our happy places say something about us. About how we recharge or what we crave.

I want a cottage on a boulder mountain. A bed and a quilt and an old stove with a teakettle on it. A telescope and a chart of constellations. Books everywhere. Removed from the world but also in it, caring about it and for it. Being old and thoughtful with a pipe to smoke on the porch and a few squirrels who trust me. A raven would be even better. And friends stopping in. Nieces and nephews making the trek to the mountain for a night of stories and some whiskey in their Dr Pepper. I'll pour it and say, "This never happened."

Of course, I'm too social for that fantasy. I like being in the thick and churn of society. So I'd probably get up to that cabin on a mountain and leave after a month or two. But who knows what age will do to me. Who knows if I'll slow down, less hungry and more content. Who knows if I'll find a raven who'll have me.

When I am off trail,
And I see a flower in the woods,
Clinging to the edge of a boulder,
Perhaps it blooms only for a week,
I think, "I am probably the only person who will ever see this flower."

There feels to be an injustice there. Beauty wasted or something.

As if the measure of something's worth is observation. Or accolade.

Maybe that is our one true job, to see the little showings, the show-offs, because we may be the only one who says "Good job, little one!"

Or maybe it doesn't matter. Maybe the ultimate lesson is this: All is vanity! Don't seek to be seen. Be beautiful anyway. Because it serves a different purpose. The bee will see. That is enough.

The world is beautiful in every tiny unseen place.

Right now, a trillion flowers are blossoming in unseen forests. They will never be seen. Right now it's happening.

But anyway, "Ahhh, I have so many messages to respond to. What will happen if I drop the ball! Will he text back? Am I pretty?"

Such funny creatures. Bloom to bloom.

Friendship

It is difficult to get a permit to raft through the Grand Canyon. For decades, there was a waitlist. You would put in your name, and the National Park Service would say, "Current wait time is twenty years." In 2006, they switched to a lottery system that they still use today. This means you *could* win every year, or you could enter every year forever and never get picked at all. Chances of getting picked for a summer slot are less than 1 percent. It adds a bit of magic to being selected. As if the river chose you.

There are ways, however, to boost your luck. If you get picked, you become a "trip leader" and get to invite fifteen people on "your" trip. So, if you get fifteen friends to apply, your chances go way up. If you've never been, or you haven't been on a trip in ten years, your name gets put in the pot five times. The more newbies you can get to apply, the better.

I didn't know any of this when I was invited to go. I knew only that it was a once-in-a-lifetime kind of thing. The most epic three-week trip in the United States. Camping on secluded beaches surrounded by giant red cliffs a billion years old. Stumbling upon Native American ruins and paintings. Bathing in the ancient Colorado River and dancing under the stars. I heard that most people would never be chosen, so if someone invites you to go on their trip, you should go. Even if you hate them. Just go.

Luckily, these were dear friends of mine. My most adventurous friends. My friend Toby—the doctor who coached me through my illness that summer—is the one who got the permit. Leslie, his wife, is an environmental consultant, lobbying for salmon habitats and ecoliteracy. They have ridden horses across Mongolia and biked across Korea, Japan, and Patagonia. They're *those* people. Doers and big adventurers. And their crew of friends teems with memory makers and say-yesers. Among them, Whitney, my old roommate and the source of all of them in my life, who somehow holds a big-boss job while always seeming to be camping on a distant cliff. They're the type of friends who will take three weeks off from work in March to raft the Colorado. All of them. And if their employers get pissy about it, they'll quit.

I'd hung out with them in San Francisco and liked them a lot, but I was surprised when they asked me to join their trip. I was in the friend group, but not core. I was very flattered. Maybe they did it because they knew of my big bike trip, or because I'm as positive and averse to confrontation as a golden retriever puppy. When you're trapped with sixteen people at the bottom of a canyon, group dynamics become paramount. Toby and a few of his friends had been lucky enough to do the trip before, and they said bad vibes had tainted the memory. Egos and annoyance and drunken make-out sessions that led to caught feelings and thick air. There was no escape—nothing to do but tolerate or shut down.

The trip downriver takes twenty-one days. Completely off the grid. They give you a satellite phone to check the weather or call a helicopter if someone snaps a femur. You pack twenty-one days' worth of food. Twenty-one days of booze. Twenty-one days of toilet paper. And on that note, you shit in boxes and carry it with you. The trip is absolutely "leave no trace." The dump you took on the first morning will stay with you until the last. If the weather's right, you sleep on a mat under the stars. If it's not right, you sleep in the tent you packed.

We left on a Friday morning. An outfitter company called Ceiba put the trip together for us. The boats we rented, the dry suits that you wear while going through rapids, the shit boxes, the toilet setup, called "the groover," and basically all the food. They plan out your meals down to the appetizer and entrée. The launch point is a section of the Colorado River just south of Glen Canyon Dam, in a modest canyon in Navajo country that would hardly inspire a postcard. I had trouble believing that just downriver from here was the most epic water-carved land on planet Earth.

We pulled up and saw our five inflated rubber boats on the riverbank. Huge rafts, like the rescue boats you'd see hanging off the back of a ferry. A white cargo truck opened its back door to reveal three weeks' worth of food and booze, all impeccably organized in gigantic coolers. Packing all this food and alcohol and tents and sleeping bags and clothes onto five boats seemed like some sort of pipe dream. (When asked to preorder booze for yourself for three weeks, every single person orders enough for a full ten-year apocalypse.) The stuff looked like it needed a transpacific barge. Yet through a feat of extraordinary jigsawing, the boats were packed.

There was a clear hierarchy to our group, with Toby at the top. He had the satellite phone. He got to be the last word on how many miles we'd go each day and when we'd take rest days (usually once a week). He was the only one who looked at the weather and the map. Then came the four other boat captains, one for each of the other boats. All of them had some level of white-water rafting experience. Some grew up doing it. Some had gone down a river just once. It was their job to know what was on their boat and where, and to strap it all down each morning as we took off. Second to last came the passengers who had rafted before. Their expertise allowed them to mother the final lot: me and the few other newbies. We were there to be bossed around, to lean into our ignorance, and give those with more experience the chance to feel not only needed, but wise.

Toby divided the sixteen of us into four teams. One out of every four days, he explained, your team would make everyone's breakfast and dinner, set up the lunchtime sandwich station, set up the groover at the night's campsite, and then tear it all down and pack it onto the boats in the morning. Then, the other three days, you let the other teams serve you.

We launched at midday from the shore and paddled through the humble beginnings of the canyon. Setting off put a spirit in my chest. A confirming, affirming swell. I was on an adventure, but not alone. I was part of a capable team. A nomadic family. A community.

It got me thinking about what community actually is. Everyone wants it. Countless organizations say they offer it. Many people still go to church almost exclusively because of it. But where does community come from? I don't think it springs from simple proximity. Most Americans don't know their neighbors. There has to be an organizing principle. A gravity point. A reason why people are drawn together. It can be intentional, like with church, or circumstantial, like at a job. But communities always form for a reason, and that reason bears greatly on the type of community that's created.

Not long ago, I went to hear Cheryl Strayed and Elizabeth Gilbert speak at UCLA. The auditorium was buzzing with energy. With writers and creatives. My friend remarked, "Everyone in here seems so nice and sweet. Look at their glowing faces!"

"Anyone who wants to hear these women speak is probably good-hearted," I said.

At one point in the evening, Elizabeth Gilbert brought it up. "I hope you'll take a moment and meet the people sitting next to you. If you're here, you're probably pretty like-minded and probably awesome. Make a new friend today." When the evening was over, people stood in the aisles and talked and laughed and hugged.

I think a lot of people lack positive community because they don't pay attention to the gravity points in their life. They don't seek out places that would attract the people they want to be surrounded by. Do you only know people from partying? From chance encounters or co-worker proximity? Not all communities are equal. A violent mob is one kind of community. So is a mean-spirited lunch table of bullies. Those communities will satiate one part of the human need for tribe, but they will kill another: the need to be proud of who you are.

Positive community is always formed around a group mission. Whether it's beautifying a neighborhood or winning a political campaign or spreading the Gospel, there is always something forming the community outside of the desire for community. It is a by-product of purpose, not a purpose in and of itself. We need to find places of attraction that attract the human beings we want to be. Maybe it's church. Maybe it's volunteer work. Maybe it's a hiking club or an architecture tour. Either way, when we find these places, we must talk to the people there.

As our group floated into the canyon, I felt the clearest sense of community I have ever known. All the complexities were stripped down to a tribal scenario: sixteen people against a river. Sixteen people vetted for positivity and aptitude. Sixteen people who knew the spiritual salve of feeling small amid the bigness of nature.

Our purposes: Make it downriver. Enjoy the beauty. Hike. Get drunk. Leave no trace. Learn about the people who lived here ten thousand years ago. Avoid drowning in the big rapids. Wear costumes. Sleep under the sky. As we moved into the canyon, the walls shot up. What had been a few hundred feet of cliff became a thousand.

We had a book that explained the different layers of rock. As the Colorado dug out the American landscape on its way to the ocean, it unearthed bands of sediment that hadn't seen the sun in a billion years. The rim of the canyon is Kaibab limestone, which is roughly 270 million years old. Below it, eleven more layers of rock, with names like Surprise Canyon Formation and Muav. They date back to as many as 550 million years ago, each one a different color and a relic of an epoch that makes human history feel like a fart in the wind. After that, there's a division in the rock called the Great Unconformity. Below that point, the rock leaps in age to over 700 million years. In some places, it's 1.8 billion years old. This is obviously when aliens harvested all of earth's crust for some ghastly project. The oldest layer, called Vishnu Basement Rocks, is as far as the Colorado has carved. Who knows what it will reveal in millions more years.

Being in the presence of age like that . . . it does something to you. You *feel* perspective. The air flexes with nature's royalty. And when you're experiencing it with fifteen friends, all submerged in that profundity, it cements the bond. As we made our way through rapids, and lunch spots, and hikes to ancestral ruins, we moved like an organism. We would pull the boats up to a campsite in midafternoon, after about five or six hours of river. The four people on dinner duty would pick their tent sites first, while the rest of us waited by the boats like a pride of lions honoring the established eating order. Once the kitchen crew had chosen the best spots, we would help unload the tables and the pots and pans. Then someone from the kitchen crew would "go shopping." They'd take the binder with each night's dinner plan and sort through the boats' coolers for whatever meat and vegetables and snacks and appetizers were needed.

Each of us had been asked to bring a "specialty cocktail" to make while the kitchen crew worked on dinner. Some people made old-fashioneds. Others made gin and tonics. We had palomas with mezcal and (somehow) fresh grapefruit slices. During the cocktail hour, someone would build the fire pit while another found firewood. Someone would go off to a secluded spot, preferably with a view, to set up the groover. Everyone chatted while working, cocktails in hand, as the sun and temperature dropped.

By the fifth night we were a machine, choreographed ants going through the effortless motions of building our portable city. The clarity of everyone's job, the sense of being needed and seeing the immediate product of our labor, was satisfying. When we slept after the day's journey, the work of setting up, and hours of storytelling and booze, we slept hard. The desert night air was cold in our nostrils. When you woke up to pee, the stars were so close, it was like bumping your head on a chandelier.

People often talk about "the way we evolved." Whether it's popular diets, exercise regimens, or theories for why humans act in the way we do, the allure of getting back to our evolutionary roots is a common selling point. We shouldn't be eating refined carbohydrates that our bodies didn't evolve to digest. We shouldn't be sedentary. Monogamy isn't natural. Should we actually be barefoot all the time? It all circles around this idea of primal humankind. The way we "were" for millions of years before history was written down, before nature was tamed and paved and air-conditioned.

I don't know what's true and what's marketing, but I can tell you this: Being in a small group of people with clear purpose and direction, with delineated roles that brought direct benefit to the group, with the flexibility to change or adapt, and with enough intimacy that social pressure could correct sour behavior . . . it felt like I was being human on the deepest level. An elemental, smooth-functioning humanity that I don't usually experience in our complex, anonymous society.

Each day we would run into some rapids. A few days we had big ones. We put on helmets and made sure every water bottle and lunch box was strapped down. Each boat captain handled the rapids differently. Some made jokes, but kept their eyes on the water like hunting owls. Some became dead serious, calling out danger spots to the boats behind them. Of greatest concern were "holes": spots where the water rushes over a large, submerged boulder to create a sudden, swirling depression. A deadly churning. It is there that a boat can be sucked down and flipped, launching the people into the air or shoving them to the river floor. More than seven hundred people have died on the river since they started counting in the mid-1800s.

As we approached a rapid, I would make loud jokes. I loved the adrenaline. My friend Whitney was frightened. She would get quiet and hunch down and say very little. I hoped my frivolous joy lightened her mood. When our boat made it through each one, the camaraderie was buzzing. We'd survived something together. We'd worked as a group, protected one another. We popped beers and drank rosé from a bag.

Most everyone on the trip did the full three weeks. I was only able to do eight days. Not because I'm a city slicker or weak or afraid of rapids, but because I had a writing job that I couldn't miss. There is a point, eight days deep into the canyon, a billion years into the rock, where a hiking trail reaches the Colorado from the rim above. It is called Phantom Ranch. From there, it is a ten-mile hike, gaining four thousand feet of elevation, from hot sun hitting the river to cold snow at the rim. When we planned the trip, two other people needed to leave early, so we coordinated with three friends to hike down from the rim on the night before we left. They were replacing us, making sure the machine kept functioning properly. There could be no missing pieces.

As we ascended those massive cliffs, watching geology change from the core of the earth to the crowded vegetation and bustle of the higher layers, I felt myself return to the busyness of modern humans. My phone buzzed for the first time in eight days. News had happened. I'd forgotten about the president and the trade war with China. People had invited me to birthdays and dinners. People had sent me memes. I felt immediately overwhelmed by the amount of information I had grown so accustomed to digesting. Some warm animal in me, which had finally come out to play on the river, retreated to his deep hole in the ground.

ONLY IN THE last several hundred years has the average person been able to write a letter and send it to someone far away. Then, in the last two hundred years, came the ability to talk instantly across large expanses.

I remember using AOL Instant Messenger in college to tell a friend I was gay. This was before texting became commonplace. I remember feeling the historical weirdness of it in the moment. In the past, I would have written her a letter, and she would've had the night to sleep on what she read. To ponder her words and choose them. And then I would've had days of wondering and growing and processing myself. But here we were, in 2002, typing instantly back and forth to each other. She was responding in real time, but I didn't have the richness of seeing her face, of being in her presence, of tempering my words with tone and fear and a shaky voice. She was reading cold black letters from a thousand miles away. I remember her spinning. Getting upset. And I couldn't console her. I tried calling, but she didn't answer. I thought, "Never in history has instant, distant writing been possible. This is a new thing."

The itch to have friends—to engage with and be valued and seen by another person—gets scratched through the Internet. Internet friendship is something, in the same way that masturbation is something; it feels good and serves a purpose. But it is not sex. Pornography is not sex, either, and might even deform real sex. By giving us the visual piece of it for cheap and keeping the hard and relational and tangible parts withheld, it can make us expect one form of ecstasy without important contextualization. Social media may be similar in this way.

Don't get me wrong, I love social media and I love the Internet. I have friends on Instagram and Twitter—real friends whom I've never met and never will. These things have value, and maybe they will bring us an altogether new type of relationship. But for now, we are physical creatures with a billion years of social wiring that includes physical presence. Time spent together. Touch. Loyalty. Inconveniencing the self by being by the other's side, helping them move homes or go to the doctor. The undigitizable experience of togetherness, of scents in the air and tasting the same food.

The shallow scratching of text messages and notifications try to replicate the real. But I have seen how the constant buzzing of the phone, the lighting up, keeps me in the shallow plane. Holds me up top. When I'm in conversation with a friend and my phone is near, I might see a text. Now the conversation is bifurcated into two paths. I am no longer fully there with my friend before me. I am also, at least in some part, with the friend who is pinging me from afar. Something of life is lost. Some wholeness of experience. Something we crave.

Eight days in the Grand Canyon was such a short reprieve from the connected world. But it reached into me through my mouth and took hold of my spine, and rattled me. I hadn't felt so simply alive in years. Most important, I really noticed.

THERE ARE SEVERAL types of friendships, but two main categories: circumstantial and kindred. The first kind happens among co-workers or classmates. They're around you for a reason, and you have fun times and good laughs. But you aren't cut from the same cloth. A kindred friend is different, someone who is on the same journey as you through life. Whether it's creative ambition, a spiritual bent, or a way of seeing the world, you find that you speak the same language and are fixated on the same books. You are headed to the same distant hill. One that no one else can see.

In tenth grade I had a realization that changed my life. A new girl named Joy came to our school and sat in front of me in Mr. Wagner's chemistry class. She was cool, funny, and smart. She thought I was, too, even though she spoke like a worldly adult and I seemed to speak like a child. She didn't seem to notice that I was weird and awkward. She was kind to me. We would sit in her car and she would play me Radiohead songs. We talked about family and life and God.

I remember my young brain was so confused. To that point, I had only had friends who picked on me. They were smart and funny guys, but we were kids—nothing was serious, sarcasm was king, and my chubby cheeks and earnest enthusiasm were an easy target. But this new girl, she treated me completely differently. She made me see that there were friends out there who would be kind and make me a better

person. I realized I wasn't stuck. That life is about who you're around. Your sense of self is built or broken by the company you keep. Thank you, Joy, for teaching me that.

Around that time, I read Thomas Merton and became fixated on his idea that "you are made in the image of what you desire." So I sought out people with integrity, cleverness, a sense of awe at the world, a lack of cynicism. If you desire friends only to appease your hunger for popularity, you'll feed that monster. But if you seek good people, wise people— not just to be associated with them, but to be good and wise yourself—I believe you will find them.

As I've gotten older, maintaining friendships has become a choice and a challenge. When I was in high school and college, friendships were propped up by convenience, although I didn't know it then. We saw one another every day because we were in the halls together, or on campus. It wasn't a choice. We were shoved into a school with hundreds of people, and we found the ones we liked. We shared gripes about teachers, about relationships, about family.

When school is over, you might be lucky enough to work somewhere with co-workers that you like. Maybe you see them every day and have inside jokes and it's all good. But lots of people don't have that. And the friendships you built in school take a lot of energy to maintain. Maybe your friends have moved away, or you have, or things have changed.

Each year, I go camping with some guys I've been friends with for more than a decade. They've got wives and a few of them have kids. We're at different stages of family, faith, philosophy, and career. Our paths crossed for a season and then we went. But with a rare few humans in life, the urge to maintain overpowers the canyon of inconvenience. And you find yourself making plans.

On our last trip, camping at the foot of the eastern Sierras, we talked about surrendering to life's seasons. About sex, society, and poetry. We cooked our meals and stumbled back to our tents in the dark after too much whiskey. I took two puffs of a joint and laughed so hard trying to tell a joke that I cried and fell into a bush.

THERE ARE ELEMENTS I look for in friendship:

Curiosity. The attraction to knowing what is true in spite of attachment to something already believed.

Kindness and mischief. A foundational generosity toward others, but not in the way of the pious martyr who cannot laugh at the weirdness of people. I need you to love all, but smack their back and say "Damn, you act a fool sometimes!" Laughing at the world and yourself in equal measure.

Belief. In something. In mystery, or humanity, or God, or the beautiful bigness of space. Nihilists and critics make me tired.

Awe. If you see the Milky Way on a clear night in the desert and don't gasp—if I point out a flower growing impossibly in the crack of cement, and you don't look—I will annoy you.

Absurdity. If you don't think God, sex, death, poop, or pain can ever be funny or absurd, I will offend you and you will wear me out in your uptightness. I'm in this life for the long haul, and need the stamina of satire and absurdity to make it through. I need to laugh with my sinister friends to survive.

Self. I need you to believe that you are worth the effort of exposition, of excavation, of education. That you matter and have something to give this world. It's okay if you don't know right now, or often forget. But I need you to believe it in there somewhere. I want to grow with you. To be sharpened by you as I sharpen you.

MY FRIEND CARLY has to leave parties sometimes. It's hard for me to understand. She'll be doing fine and then, all of a sudden, flip. "I need to go home." She says she absorbs the energy of everyone around her. She feels it all. She works in fashion, and her job sometimes requires that she attend influencer events. All that thirsty ambition and peacocking is like putting a fork in the wall socket.

When Carly was young, her mother had been a grab bag of emotions. Each morning as a little girl, Carly would wake up and come downstairs and not know which mother she would be getting. Angry. Happy. Depressed. Manic. So she learned to tread with care. She would come downstairs ready to become whoever she had to be to keep the peace. In order to survive. Now, as an adult, she can't help but walk into a room and feel it all.

I am not sensitive to the room. I am a steady, smiling dog who wags his tail wherever he goes. But that often diminishes my empathy, my work as a friend. Someone will say, "What's wrong with Ryan?" and I'll be like, "What? Nothing. He seemed fine to me." And then I find out he's crying in the bathroom.

Many of my closest friends have the opposite, a radius of the heart that reaches out and feels the beating of others. My friend Ruthie is like that, a human energy sponge. She feels the room in a way I do not.

She and I were talking about this one day, and I got insecure about my dark robotic heart. "Maybe this makes me a bad person," I said. "I don't notice other people's feelings."

She stopped me. "It can be a good thing, Jed. Sometimes when people feel shitty, they don't want to dwell on it. They don't want to be treated like fragile glass. They want to feel normal, to be pulled out of their darkness. You treat everyone the same. Your energy is constant. Like every day is a new chance to be amazed. That can help people."

Ruthie knows about human feelings. She's had to study her own for twenty years. At seventeen, she was T-boned in a car accident and broke her neck, permanently damaging her brain stem. For the last few decades, she has lived with chronic pain that I cannot comprehend. The broken nerves tell her brain that she is being ripped in half, all day, every day. She describes it as half of her body being on fire. Other forms of pain don't register. She has found herself standing on a fire-ant hill, her leg brown with ants, all biting her. She had no idea.

For most of her twenties, Ruthie was bedridden, taking the highest legal dose of fentanyl every day. Then, her world fell apart. Her beloved father collapsed and died. She was married at the time, and her husband couldn't take it. He left her. She decided she couldn't keep going as she was, a burning human pile of drugs and loss. She decided to wean herself off all the medicine. Better to live in pain than live as a zombie. She started drinking alcohol at age thirty-three.

She had never been sexual with anyone other than her husband. She was, in many ways, so similar to me. Feeling like her twenties had been some kind of testing ground or desert, rich in pain but also in teaching.

I seek Ruthie's counsel for all kinds of things, but especially interpersonal things. She is a student of her own mind, and her pain has given her a superhuman capacity to meet people where they hurt. To sit beside them in silence. In my comparatively monotone emotional experience, she colors the gray.

As I beat myself up that day, she gave me perspective on the different roles we play. "I do what I do, and it can help. You do what you do, and it can help. Some days we need a comforter. Some days we need perspective. Some days we need to stop staring in the mirror asking why, and go outside and be amazed at the world. Some days we need a kick in the ass."

This framing clicked for me.

In Christianity, there's an idea called the Body of Christ. Some of us are hands, while others are feet. Some ears and some mouths. If a foot sat around wishing it were the mouth, the body would never move. Every part has a function; until it finds its place in the wholeness, the body is incomplete.

I am not porous. I don't feel the room, and that's because I'm usually not in it. I am thirty thousand feet up. I see everything from above, and usually see it popping into the puzzle, completing some new part. This is why I write. To process what I see up there. Meanwhile, there are people in the room, holding hands, listening to each other with tears in their eyes. They are feeling everything. And they are saving hearts.

We are parts of the big body of the world. You have a role. So do I. That weirdness in you is the very thing some-one needs.

EVER NOTICE HOW you can watch a press conference, and at the smallest squint of an eye, the subtlest tone of voice or word choice, your gut says, "He's lying!" Or do you ever go on a first date, and in the free flow of good conversation, you notice that his knee touched yours under the table, per-haps for .02 seconds instead of .01? The latter could have been an accident, but the former felt like exploratory affec-tion. It registers immediately. Meanwhile, above the table, you're still talking about *Broad City.*

Our brains are primed for social interaction. More than anything else, it's the skill that makes us human.

Our schools and our tests look for aptitude in skills that can be measured and tallied. Whether we're good at calculus or chemistry, for example. But this leaves out many a bril-liant mind. I remember people from my high school who struggled to make B's and C's, but were social savants. So-cial interactions? Human nuance? They knew every detail. But numbers and statistics and facts wouldn't stick in their minds. The tests and the pressure around memorization were brutal for them, so they failed and flunked or begged and scraped by. But when class let out, they ran the school with relationship advice and gossip and perfectly timed wit. They could maneuver a conversation or convince a teacher to give them a B like Rachmaninov playing the piano.

I guess what I'm saying is, some of the most obvious geniuses I've ever met would never have scored high on the SAT. And I hate that they don't know how smart they are.

I've seen someone craft a text message conversation between their friend and the friend's crush that should be studied by science. The nuance. The empathy. The imagined perspective and channeled flirtatious energy. The impossibly perfect word choices. The fullness of the evolved human brain computing ten thousand emotions and expectations in a millisecond, and launching the text like a sniper's bullet. It's genius at work.

WHEN I WAS a kid in church, the Sunday school teachers would say, "Jesus died for you. Don't you feel loved? Don't you just feel so grateful to Jesus?" I would think to myself, "I mean, I guess . . . but he loves everyone, which means I'm not special. And if he didn't die for us, he'd be alone in heaven. So it all kind of makes sense."

But as I've gotten older, the tables have been turned. I've always been told, "You love everyone. You make everyone feel uniquely seen." I spread myself around. I enjoy most people and can stay up all night talking to someone I just met. I've had dear friends say to me, "How do I know if I'm special to you? Everyone thinks they're special to you."

There is a love that is abundance, that is never diminished, a love of humanity and the celebration of every beautiful thing. And there is a love that is scarcity, of choosing you over everyone else. Of feeling special. Both kinds of love matter.

I don't know which one is better. Or if this ties into the

idea that we are all parts of the body of the universe. Some of us love everyone. Some of us choose only a few.

To be clear, I don't *looooove* everyone. I am just interested in everyone. I'll have a conversation and learn. I'll pay attention to them. And attention is often withheld from people. They feel invisible. So me noticing them, talking to them, asking follow-up questions—it can feel like love, even if it's more a by-product of my curiosity. I suppose I am kind, but I'm not sure. How many personality traits masquerade as virtue?

I've known people for years who still make me think "Who are you really? I'm not sure." On the other hand, I've met people at parties who felt like old friends after one cocktail and a story about their trip to Trader Joe's. What is that? Where does that sense of connection come from?

Some part of it is a chemical attraction—a mess of algorithms behind our consciousness that make these connections without our permission. We don't choose them; they just happen. Our animal soul recognizes another soul of its same kind and lights up. I couldn't tell you how a magnet works, but I know how it feels when one pulls.

Language has something to do with it. I've had strangers come up to me in coffee shops who know me only from reading my stories on their cellphones. When they walk up and introduce themselves, we always hug. It's all very spooky and fun. I am part of them, because something I wrote happened to speak to whoever it is they are. And I always like them, too. We're the same in the important ways.

All we want is for someone to know we exist and say, "I'm glad you're here."

Try this today. Tell a friend you're happy they're here, that you're happy to know them. Tell them it's amazing to live with them floating on this rock in space. Maybe you'll catch them as they stop to get groceries. Remind them a supernova is eating a solar system somewhere at this very moment as they put bananas in their basket. It's happening right now.

RECENTLY I WAS emailing with my friend Tom. He's been a source of wisdom and love to me for years. And he loves thinking out loud about what life means. I love how he thinks, and how he makes me think.

"When I am with you," he wrote, "the conversation moves so fast that I often must simply 'mark' a certain thought and allow the conversation to continue without speaking to it. And one such thought was when you said: 'And it made me cry, not because it is sad, but because it is so true. Truth makes me cry.'

"In my old age, I have been experiencing THAT very, very frequently. I do not understand it well—I only 'feel' it— and those around me must think it very, very odd. I cry daily, never because I am sad. Often because I care deeply. But usually just because something so profoundly true or authentic has pierced me, and experiencing the weight of that Truth or authenticity overwhelms me."

I knew exactly how Tom felt. Tears are the swelling of something inside me, until that something gets too big for my body to hold. It makes room by pushing the tears out. In a movie, when a kid who has been bullied stands up for himself, or his friends show up for him, it makes me cry. Triumph makes me cry, too.

Maybe you're in a season of crying because you're moving to Rwanda from Chicago, far away from everyone you know. Maybe some big loss or change is taking up the space in your head, and it's pushing tears out. Maybe this is the scene in the movie where the whole audience is crying, moved by the life you're living, what you've seen and done and are trying to make room for now.

WE AREN'T MEANT to go it alone. We are clueless pack animals, clawless and pretty weak as far as animals go. Our bodies surrendered their power to our brains a million years ago. But it wasn't just exchanging claws for big brains. It was what we did with those brains. In particular: cooperation.

How do humans cooperate in such huge numbers? How do we agree on money, on nations, on staying in the driving lane? Other mammals can't organize in groups larger than a few hundred. The thing that sets us apart from the other animals is our ability to believe in things. The wiring in our brains mutated in such a way that they gained the ability to hold concepts covering giant, abstract numbers of people. With language, we can construct unifying ideas like religion and country. Though I've never met you, you and I are French; therefore, we are brothers. You and I are Catholic; therefore, we are sisters. And we spread these constructs through stories we tell ourselves. Words that organize what we observe and experience.

One human would come to a wide river or bay and stop. On her own, she would be stumped by the natural barrier. But give her a tribe, a language, and a common desire—and she can build the Golden Gate Bridge. She can land on the moon. Or start a war.

Next time you're making inside jokes with your friends, take note: You are exercising a superpower. You are casually engaging in the skill that took over the world, and could someday destroy it.

MY FRIEND ZACH once said, "One person, in a million lifetimes, could never build a car."

"Think about it. One person couldn't do it. Mining the materials, the metal from mountains, copper, steel, the rubber from trees; digging up oil and refining it to gasoline; melting sand into glass for the windows; tanning leather; learning how levers and gears and motors turn; combustion engines, spark plugs . . . In a million lifetimes, one human couldn't do all the things necessary to build even one car."

Humans make things. They build and expand and astonish. Each ant has his specialty, and we all add our single brick to the skyscraper.

Exploring New York reminds me of this more than any other place. A human masterpiece built on a forest and a field and a swamp. Stone and metal and materials shipped here from Chile, Congo, Brazil, stacked together, sewn into each other. Humans born in every corner of the world, drawn here as if by Devils Tower, a city like an anthill after it's been kicked. Swarming and repairing and building.

I HATE GETTING rides from other people. What if I want to leave the dinner before my friend? What if I want to up and go somewhere else? I like my freedom. On top of that, I don't like asking for things because my worst nightmare is to appear needy. Or worse, a freeloader.

Youth can trick you into believing you are autonomous. You need no one. You are strong and free and will bounce when dropped.

Last summer, I picked up some mystery virus that knocked me on my ass. I lost my appetite and could hardly stand in the shower. I went to multiple doctors and they took lots of my blood and piss and stool and couldn't figure out what it was. I tried to play it down. Order Postmates and do it on my own. But I couldn't. I couldn't even walk to the end of the street.

I spent twelve days on the couch and in my bed. Five days in, I couldn't look at Instagram anymore, because the sight of people enjoying their lives made me sad. I wished I could teleport to Tennessee and let my mom take care of me.

But as soon as I grew too weak to protest, my friends and roommates swooped in like buzzards on a sick cow. They circled ahead until my knees buckled and I couldn't do it on my own. They made me bone broth. They brought me groceries and Gatorade and food and multivitamins and blankets and soup. When I was too weak to use my hands, I had dozens of pairs around me. When I lost my clarity to choose, I had a swarm of backup brains.

They say the average American does not have $500 saved in case of an emergency. That is not good. But man, I hope the average American has friends. Because bad things happen, and while you can live much of your life as a loner, there will come a time when you need help. To feel that warm rush of care when you've given all you've got and you fall to your knees—it is, I don't know . . . some core-ground-level thing. A confirmation from a million years ago that we were meant to lean on each other. That accepting help is not a show of weakness. It's honoring the truth that got us here: We thrive together and fail alone.

I've been to Burning Man twice. It is a massive art festival in the middle of a Nevada desert. A dry lake bed with powder-white dirt and open skies and not one tree as far as the eye can see. People camp or sleep in RVs, and spend two weeks making giant sculpture installations that dot the horizon. It is dusty, dirty, and fun. It is also a music festival and an experiment in zero-waste living. It is without question the wildest man-made thing I've ever seen. It is like stepping into a Mad Max creative explosion. It isn't for everyone, but when I went for the first time, it was definitely for me.

While wandering around on one of the last days, I stopped in a tent full of strangers to beat the midday heat. They were sitting in a circle, drinking kava tea, and taking turns explaining what they'd learned by living in the dusty desert all week. Some people talked about self-reliance; others talked about looking for love. One girl said she had come to the festival alone and ended up finding new best friends.

Then it was an older woman's turn. She was small and

fragile and leaning on a cane. She said she had mobility issues and used a battery-powered golf cart to get around. It
broke down one hour after her arrival. And when you can't
really walk, getting around a pop-up city of seventy thousand people is very difficult.

"This was my first time coming to Burning Man," she
said. "So many people told me not to come. They told me it
was too hard." . . . She started crying. "I broke down on the
first day. The dirt. The heat. I had a full meltdown. My cart
didn't work. I couldn't get anywhere on my own." But in her
despair, angels appeared. "Strangers started picking me up,
pulling me in wagons behind their bikes, placing me on their
scooters and buggies, and taking me wherever I wanted to
go. They invited me to explore with them. Go deep out into
the playa and see the art. Everywhere I turned, I was offered
help."

By this point in the story, the woman was crying so hard
the words barely made it out. That week, she had seen art
and dance parties and impromptu dinners, all because of the
generosity of strangers. Her feelings of inadequacy, the injustice of her damaged legs, of her damn golf cart breaking
down, had been met with jubilant kindness.

As I sat listening to her speak, I felt my own strong legs
folded beneath me on the bench. I hadn't even thought about
them, about what a gift it was to wander at my whim, to
hop on my bike and explore in any direction. It reminds me
of something I once heard a pastor say: "There is someone
in a hospital right now begging and praying for the chance
to live one day like you're living right now."

I don't know what is fair and what isn't. I didn't earn my
health, and I don't think this old lady earned her infirmity.

But I know that the love she felt was good, and that the privilege of ability is meant to be used for helping.

I MAY THINK that someone has the perfect life, and therefore doesn't need encouragement. Or I may see that they have it bad, but I don't want to bother them or offend them by saying the wrong thing. Either way, I assume things and stay quiet.

A friend of mine is a famous writer. He's had big success and won awards and been on TV. He told me once: "When something major happens, no one texts me to say congratulations or tells me they're excited for me. Except for my team, the people I pay. They tell me. I think my friends assume everyone else is doing that, so they don't. It sucks to achieve your dreams and feel more alone than when you were scraping by with the guys."

Another friend of mine had his brother go to prison. It was a big deal. They showed it on the news and everything. I didn't call my friend because I thought he'd be so embarrassed. I didn't want to let on that I knew. A year later, I found out that through that whole horrible ordeal, no one called him. He said he'd never felt so alone. In his time of need, no one showed up, because everyone assumed someone else was doing it.

You know that poster at the airport that says, "If you see something, say something"? That's become my motto. If somebody is killing it, I'm going to tell them. If they're hurting, I'll offer my hand. I am not going to assume anyone else exists but me and them. No one who would do what I'd do to make my friend feel seen.

. . .

MORE THAN TWO hundred years ago, Adam Smith wrote
that if a European were to hear of a terrible earthquake that
destroyed the Chinese empire, he might "express very
strongly his sorrow for the misfortune of that unhappy people." But he would undoubtedly go about his day and fall
asleep without struggle that night. "If he was to lose his little
finger to-morrow, he would not sleep to-night; but, provided
he never saw them, he will snore with the most profound
security over the ruin of a hundred millions of his brethren,
and the destruction of that immense multitude seems plainly
an object less interesting to him, than this paltry misfortune
of his own."

This was before the Internet and television, of course, so
the broadcast of faraway pain would have been limited to a
newspaper story. To the imagination. The European wouldn't
have seen crying faces or heard the voices of children. But he
certainly would have known it was the death of millions of
people. This is a moral disaster, but a feature of the human
brain. Humans don't care well for things they can't see and
feel. We didn't evolve with a global mind.

Luis Moreno Ocampo, a renowned human rights lawyer,
told me that an empathic response is more likely to be activated by three things: closeness in space, closeness in time,
and likeness to self. It's difficult to feel empathy for cave-
men, because they were different from us, lived very long
ago, and inhabited a world unlike our present life in our
present suburb. Zero for three. The wiring for empathy isn't
triggered. If you are white, from a white world and a white
suburb, and the suffering child is Chinese from a town you

cannot pronounce, your empathic response will be diminished. This is our wiring, formed from a million years of not seeing any tribe that lived more than a hundred miles away.

I believe in a global world. In global compassion. In free markets and equal human dignity. But, man, our little monkey brains really strain to process the world. They didn't evolve to do this. Which is why we fight like we do. We're too big for our britches.

NINE OUT OF ten people would murder a stranger by pulling a lever. This we know from a famous thought experiment in ethics, often called the trolley problem. Here's the scenario:

Imagine you're standing on a bridge, watching a runaway train speed down the track below. Down on the track are five unsuspecting, innocent people who will be run over—it's too late for the train to stop. But right in front of you is a lever. If you pull it, the train will switch to a different track, where only one innocent person is standing. Would you pull the lever, effectively killing the one guy to save the five, or do nothing at all? Nine out of ten people would pull it.

It gets more interesting, though, when you change the setup. Same scenario, but this time there's no switch. Instead, you're standing next to a stranger. This poor schmuck is just standing on the bridge, not paying attention, while the five people wait down on the track. Here comes the train. It will hit and kill the five when it passes beneath you. But if you push the stranger off the bridge, he'll land on the tracks and stop the train. (This is assured to you by the psychologists who created the scenario; just go with it.) If you knew the simple act of shoving the schmuck would save five lives, would you push him? Nine out of ten people say no. Hell no.

What's the difference? Same math. Same loss of life. The only difference is the lever.

Psychologists have observed that humans are deeply averse to violence when it's face-to-face. We have a deep instinct to avoid it. But remove them by one step, and that instinct is almost completely diminished. (I first heard all of this on the *Radiolab* podcast's episode "Morality." It's a must listen.)

To me, this explains why bullying thrives on the Internet. Why road rage exists more than sidewalk rage. Why drone strikes are ordered by presidents of both parties, and why governments waste money that isn't theirs. Our animal brains have no software for a world of buttons and levers and screens to hide behind.

ANYTHING BEYOND YOUR relational and experiential world is religion. It's secondhand belief. You're gluten free—do you actually know what gluten is and how it's metabolized, or did you trust your doctor or listen to your skinny friend? How we engage in these massive systems of belief—from the American experiment to the economy to the environment—is all hugely important. What we believe matters.

But remember, it's all religion. It's all fighting over this savior or that.

I want to find the person who knows conservatives and

progressives and people who are religious and nonreligious. Who eats with them. Who laughs with them. Only that person knows what to do next. Or maybe they don't. But at least I know they are asking real questions, seeing the world with sober eyes.

Trust your physical world more than the others. Trust the kindness of strangers on the sidewalk. You were designed for it.

SPENDING TIME WITH Ruthie is a poem. A sermon. We have such a good time together. But it isn't just laughing and eating and making playlists. It is a lot of that, but it's also conversations on philosophy, spirituality, and processing mystery. Her chronic pain rears its head now and then. She has to lie down. She can't go from dinner to a bar, because she's too tired. She comes to lunch late because she slept an hour the night before.

One time, when we were visiting Vermont, a weathered lady we met said to us, "This year, the leaves are extra bright."

"Why?" Ruthie asked, with her Louisiana accent that makes it sound like "Waaah?"

"It's because of the drought," the woman said. "The stress put on the trees brings out their brightest colors. You are very lucky to be visiting right now. The harder the year, the brighter the leaves."

I've seen this in Ruthie. She can sit with someone in their pain. She actually sits down with them and holds their hand. She doesn't rush to tell her experience. She doesn't try to explain it all away. She doesn't say, "It will be okay," or "All things have a purpose." She sits with them. She nods and says, "That's so hard," and "I'm so sorry, angel."

I am terrible at this. I tell the suffering person that everything has meaning. I try to make them laugh. I tell them it'll pass.

Ruthie teaches me the value of suffering. The cost of the brightness of our leaves. The number of times I have heard people say, "I just met Ruthie, and I am forever changed," is too many to count.

How do you let a friendship go? Solve that sad calculus of realizing you have changed, and that a person who was once your partner in crime is now a reminder of something you've left behind?

I can meet an old friend at a coffee shop for the dreaded "catch-up," and search for words and stories, always falling back on the memories of when our lives were in right flow. But our lives are no longer in the same river. We're flowing to different seas.

What of loyalty? What of remembering the old times? I think it depends on where and why you grew up. Did you find your true self when you became different from your friends? Was it freedom? Do they, even in their kindness and beautiful memories, represent ways that you used to be imprisoned?

When I sit with a kindred friend, my effortless people, there is no catching up. Everything is understood. It's an explosion of futures. It makes me wonder how many people in this world feel understood by their friends. How many people are friends with the people who happened to be around, never knowing why they feel alone in a room full of their own?

I AM DRAWN to some people from across a room, without ever having to hear their voice. They can walk into a crowd and stand out to me like a lighthouse.

When you're driving down the freeway, and someone begins driving right next to you at the same speed, you notice them peripherally. You feel them there. You look left and see them keeping perfect pace, and for that moment, you are together, speeding down the road in the same direction. That's how it feels with some friends. A same-speed recognition. A feeling of mutual momentum and direction.

And then there are people that I am drawn to precisely because they are different. Perhaps they have something I lack. I am attracted to stoics because I am extroverted confetti. I am attracted to bodies because I too often get lost in my mind. I am attracted to people who can't find the right words, because in a way, not knowing what to say is lovely to me. I am attracted to people who express and heal their pain, because I run from mine.

It dawns on me that all my relationships are just chemistry unfolding. Equations seeking equilibrium. Sameness finding sameness. And imbalance finding balance. I am water pouring down the mountain, looking for low places to rest and pool. I am meeting up with streams to form a river—and hopefully, ultimately, to join the sea.

. . .

MY FRIEND MARGIE and I have grown through many seasons together. From building youth-activist campaigns to deconstructing our Christianity. We are two very different bodies running the same software in our minds. Awhile back, we got to talking about growing up, and the way our thinking has evolved in our thirties.

She said, "All the things that used to make me mad, the Christian stuff, my parents, the exes and aging, they just 'are' now. It's like someone stole the charge right out of them."

I can't get this thought out of my head. How I used to get so fired up about things. How offended I was when someone interpreted the Bible differently than I did. How frightened I was by intimacy. How cartoonish my expectations of adulthood were. How hurt I was when someone didn't invite me. How I spent entire evenings arguing over heaven and hell, music and marriage. How certain I was, fighting for such smallness.

I see the world with different eyes now. I appreciate the time everything takes. The analogy of the orchestra returns to me. Each instrument in its own time. The spirited trumpet has his solo, but the soothing strings come next.

I wonder how I'll feel in ten years. If the growth ever stalls or stops. I've seen some people lock into a way of thinking, build their sense of safety around it, and never learn a new thing. I've also met old people who go around with a twinkle in their eye, still surprised by their own words, still delighted in their unfolding.

· · ·

You CAN'T MAKE new old friends. Unless when you meet them, your spirit jumps to your lips and shouts, "I've known you for longer than I've been alive. We are siblings from the stars."

I WAS ASKED recently, "Who is your best friend?" I don't know. I don't use language like that anymore. It doesn't fit. I have friends that hold the keys to different doors of my personality. Some open my heart. Some my laughter. Some my mischief. Some my sin. Some my civic urgency. Some my history. Some my rawest confusion and vulnerability. Some friends, who may not be "the closest" to me, have the most important key for me in a moment of my life. Some, who may be as close as my own skin, may not have what I need today. It's okay if our spouses or partners don't have every key. How could they? It isn't a failure if they don't open every single door of who you are. The million-room-mansion of identity cannot overlap perfectly with anyone.

But I will say, my closest friends have a key ring on their hip with lots of keys, jingling.

WHO DO YOU feel the most yourself with? That is a trick question. Because I am many selves. I am myself when I am with my serious friends, discussing politics and race and faith and wounds. I am myself with my playful friends, when I'm cackling at a restaurant and getting shushed by respectable adults trying to have a respectable meal. I am myself when I'm with my fearless friends, hopping fences and sneaking into parks at night. I am as many people as I meet, the hidden parts of me being pulled out by the unique alchemy of every connection.

Who do you hang with that makes you feel the fullness of one of yourselves? For me, Ruthie is a good example. She wants nothing from me but delight. She wants to laugh and talk, but she doesn't show up needing it. She knows only that mixing the ingredients of her and me make good things. We are interested in the same music, many of the same books and movies, the same cocktails and food, and the same people. Where we differ, we intrigue each other. Where we overlap, we feel understood. It's a weird thing, being around people like that. Even though it might be frantic with activity and dinners and talking, it feels like rest. There is no work. No weighing or even thought of self. No doubt. No poison of wishing you were different. You stop holding your breath. You pant like a dog.

But it is also like electricity. Energy without a battery. It requires no fuel—the friendship itself is eternal combustion. Delight and laughter and mischief spring out of everything. The smallest, dumbest thing is comedy. We find the perfect taco or cocktail and scream, "Of course!" We make a scene and strangers notice us from across the way. Their forks pause midway to their mouths as they watch with worried eyes. "Are these people about to burn this place down?"

The answer is yes.

AFTER GIVING A speech at a conference in downtown L.A., I checked my phone backstage and saw a text from my friend Sophia. "Patch is in a bad way. I'm wondering if you, my chosen family, can come over and spend the day with me and him and let's send him to heaven surrounded by the love he's given us for fourteen years."

I apologized to the organizers that I couldn't stay for the meet-and-greet and ran to my car. I had to get to Sophia's house.

Patch was a pit bull rescue with one eye. He lost the other one from a fight or abuse. No one really knows. But Sophia rescued this rejected broken dog, and he traveled with her everywhere. Though his one eye gave him a hard look, he was a cuddle puddle. A kisser and a lover. He napped in our laps and licked us clean.

When I pulled up to the house, the street was lined with cars. I had to park two blocks away. I wondered if someone else was having a party. But as I walked back up the hill, I saw that the cars were centered around Sophia's house. Once inside, I looked out the back windows into the yard. People were everywhere. I went out back and saw so many friends and dear faces, standing and watching Patch eat ice cream. I had that tight feeling in my throat that comes with tears, seeing all my friends in one place, rallied last-minute to be the love Sophia needed. To show Patch the love he deserved.

Patch couldn't walk anymore or control his functions, so on his glorious last day as a dog, they had been waiting on him, feeding and petting him like King Solomon. They fed him bacon, salami, ice cream, all the things a dog could dream of. They let him drink beer. He must've gone numb from being rubbed and petted.

When the kindhearted vet showed up, Sophia assumed most of us would leave. Who wants to watch a vet inject a dog with death? And yet everyone stayed. There were probably fifteen of us and we quieted and took the posture of reverence. Patch was given something to make him fall into the deepest, loveliest sleep. Sophia lay beside him, spooning him on his bed. She whispered things to him that I couldn't hear. She giggled. He was snoring loudly. Then, he went to be with all the dogs that have loved humans before him. We were crying.

I said to my friend Azita, "Take note. I want this when I go. I want this exact day."

There are many lonely humans who have never known the love this dog knew. He earned it by the way he loved us—but first, he was invited in to love. Sophia took a chance on him. He was a reject. He might have been mean and sad. A "dangerous dog." But Sophia said, "I will be your home. Your safe place." And he became the best dog in history. The power of the invitation.

THE WORDS "AUTHENTIC" and "community" don't mean anything on their own. Some things are meant to be by-products, not causes or aims. We are desperate for authenticity and community, and in our haste, we mistake them for goals. But these things are like friendship, like flirting, like humor: If you talk about them, they retreat like a shadow in the light. You cannot discuss pheromones while flirting and expect your knees to keep touching under the table. Some things, some beautiful things, are the smoke and not the fire.

In the same way, you cannot will community into existence. If you gather people around you and squint and smile and say, "We are such a community, how amazing are we!" watch your friends run.

BELONGING IS THE first source of invincibility. Of happiness.

I had to speak at a conference in wine country awhile ago, and I was nervous. I felt like an imposter. I can gab and chat like a pro, but an hour of giving a structured lecture makes me shiver. My friend Lauren, the one who started Kind Campaign, said, "I'll come with you and be your hype machine. A ROAD TRIP! Let's do it!"

There is something well suited about a road trip and a close friend. The ability to talk while on the move, while passing through small towns and canyons and souvenir shops. You can oscillate between personal excavation and playful observation about the things you see while driving through rural America. Lauren is excellent at this. She can talk about a supernova and then local Los Angeles politics and then my love life as if they were all related. She is a professional at locking eyes across a table with me when things get weird or precious. I feel such comfortable belonging with her. It's the confidence that comes from having a comrade, a friend whose counsel you seek and mischief you ignite.

There are things in my life that make me feel small and dumb. For example, I am a dizzy slob when it comes to my romantic life. I don't know what I'm doing or feeling, and my love of words only masks my ignorance. Lauren has a profoundly loving and balanced marriage, but she had her share of wild boyfriends and bad ideas and messy heart-aches. She is on the phone every other day talking to one friend or another about their ghosting crush, a first date, a fluttering heart, or a confusing text message. I am embarrassed by my fumblings into the dating world; she is so thrilled by it all, it makes me open up. I feel less crazy when she pats my back.

We drove hundreds of miles and spilled out our hearts and words. We played the "song biography" game, where you play key songs from your youth that impacted you. You first explain what they meant to you and why, and then you hit play. I was playing Alanis Morissette and Shane & Shane and Dave Matthews Band. She was playing Jimmy Eat World and Coldplay. We arrived at the conference feeling exfoliated and whole. I think I nailed the talk. She patted my back and said, "Good job, my dude."

I WANT TO make up a new word, or find the word for the feeling.

It will mean, "When a group of friends is in a moment, and everyone hits a harmony of laughter, or playing off each other. Where we realize in a moment, maybe at sunset at Mount Hood, or with beers around a fire, or blazing the streets at a bachelor party, that there is no other place we would rather be. Where the moment is so fat with harmony that it's both spacious and weightless, passing painfully and at the same time immortal."

.   .   .

HOW DOES SOMEONE find community? Good friends? I get asked this a lot, and I don't know how to answer. But there are clues. The friends I have all seem to have certain traits in common. Our interests overlap. We like politics and art and television and books. We are funny. There is self-sufficiency mixed with openhanded generosity. We operate from celebration and delight rather than ownership and expectation.

Then there were the gravity points. At nineteen, I moved to Los Angeles, one of the most creative cities in the world, full of creative people. I went to film school and then studied poetry in the English department. I met actors and film directors and wannabes who ended up becoming the real thing. I worked at a young nonprofit that made avant-garde documentaries about child soldiers and kids surviving a war zone. We uploaded YouTube videos and lobbied Congress and the Obama administration for human rights aid while wearing Converse sneakers. We wanted to save lives and make art while we did it. Of course I found interesting people there.

I'm thirty-seven now, so I'd say I've had about twenty years of seeking real friendships. I've lived long enough to meet loads of people and grab on to the ones who sing my soul electric. Every one of them started as a bird who landed on my shoulder. They always could've flown away. Yet many of them remain. Free as a finch to visit my shoulder or not. I enjoy them and they enjoy me. We enjoy the freedom to continue to choose one another. But I will say, I am learning the beauty of loyalty. Of history. Of having years and years of one another.

For a long time, I resisted seeing loyalty as a virtue. People who said they sought loyalty first were a red flag to me. It implied that they were trouble. Like they'd been terrible people and had so many friends pull away and leave, that now they were always talking about how many "fake" friends there are, how rare loyalty is.

But I see loyalty differently now. I see it as time-tested friendship. As weathering many seasons together, of taking one another's advice. We do stupid things, we date the wrong people or get back with the wrong ex, and yet the friendship survives. Because the connection is deeper than just enjoyment, just fun and laughs. It has become something more like family. Where it's no longer a choice, but a given.

At thirty-seven, I can feel my life getting smaller. I've found the ones I love, and now we have something that cannot be found in a flash of quick connection: We have history.

I WILL ALWAYS be fascinated by the function of friendship. C. S. Lewis said, "Friendship is unnecessary, like philosophy, like art. . . . It has no survival value; rather it is one of those things that gives value to survival." This is patently false. Of course it has survival value. It bonds us to one another, making our tribes strong enough to survive the chaos of life. It gives our social connections pleasure and stamina. It gives form to our social hierarchies, to who you can trust and who you can't. And, like anything in human life, it changes as it ages.

Friendship in my twenties was an exercise in empire building. I had an endless well of energy to meet new people, to jump at the spark of a new connection. But my priorities are switching from breadth to depth. I have collected all my flowers. I have planted them. I am now focusing on tending to my garden.

I am happy about this. And I will report back in thirty years.

Truth, like love and sleep, resents approaches that are
too intense.

—W. H. Auden

I would add friendship to this quote. You can't want it too bad or you'll poison it. That's certainly true of love.

Love

I had my first kiss on Sunday, May 1, 2011. It's easy to remember the exact date because it happened on the day we all learned Osama bin Laden had been killed. I was twenty-eight years old.

I had been in Los Angeles for the weekend and was taking the train back home to San Diego. It's a three-hour trip. I remember that I was getting into San Diego late, around ten-thirty P.M. This was before Uber, in the days when friends had to pick you up from the airport or train station.

The sky had just drifted into darkness, and I was reading a magazine in my seat on the train. The car was neither crowded nor empty, just a dozen or so people sitting quietly. At about eight forty-five P.M., a woman stood up with a sense of urgency. "Osama bin Laden has been killed!" There was a beat of silence, and then people cheered. Strangers locked eyes, saying "Wow" and "Oh my God." I checked Twitter on my phone and saw that President Obama was addressing the nation. I opened the Al Jazeera news stream, and there was the president, talking in midsentence.

". . . has conducted an operation that killed Osama bin Laden, the leader of al-Qaeda, and a terrorist who's responsible for the murder of thousands of innocent men, women, and children. It was nearly ten years ago that a bright September day was darkened by the worst attack on the American people in our history."

As I watched with my headphones in, the train disappeared. For a moment, I was purely an American. Nothing else. I was an entity inside history. Then, when the announcement ended, I took off my headphones and returned to the train. It was buzzing with energy. People were talking and reading on their phones. *Where was his body really? Would we see actual photos?*

I texted a boy named Jackson. "They killed Osama bin Laden!"

"I just saw," he wrote. "Wow!"

"In other news, would you want to pick me up from the train? I get in at 10:30 though. It's so late."

"I would love to! Can I take you to a secret beach that I love?"

"Oooh, bring a bottle of wine?"

"Yes duh. See you at 10:30, I'm excited."

I texted Jackson because I thought he might have a crush on me. This was not something I deduced on my own. "Jackson likes you," a friend had said after seeing us hang out. "No, he doesn't!" I insisted. No one had ever *liked* me. I had no metrics or experience in being crushed on. No intuition. My friend assured me I was wrong. That Jackson was all up on my steez.

I had met Jackson a few weeks earlier because a mutual friend told me I should. He worked as a student chaplain at Point Loma Nazarene University, a conservative Christian college in San Diego, and had recently come out as gay. Not only that, but unapologetically so. Gay and Christian and a leader and proud of it. The Nazarene community erupted into a torrent of controversy. *Do we fire him? He isn't acting on it . . . yet.* It divided the conservative staff and student body from the surprisingly sizable number of progressive students. Jackson was a micro-celebrity-agitator. He knew the Bible better than most. He was ready to debate anyone, and possessed a freedom I hardly knew. Someone put us on a text, and we started talking.

At twenty-eight years old, I had only just decided I was willing to date men. I'd known I was different since I was eight, and known that I was gay from age twelve. But at eighteen, I decided I wouldn't act on it until God told me I could. I didn't want to go against the plain reading of scripture. "If a man lies with a male as with a woman, both of them have committed an abomination; they shall be put to death; their blood is upon them." These aren't code words. They're clear warnings. I didn't want to weather the rejection and wrath of my entire Christian community, which included most of my friends.

A year before that train ride, I'd been in a van driving down a bumpy dirt road in Uganda when this approach started to rip me up beyond repair. I was there co-leading a tour for some of our nonprofit's donors. Taking a bunch of Americans on a ten-day trip to rural Uganda fast-tracks friendship. Lots of fireside talks and beer and sharing. Inside jokes being formed every mile. And the long drives between villages, through tall grass and unkempt mud roads, had us playing games and talking about all kinds of things.

On this stretch, everyone in the van started talking about when they had their first kiss. At age fourteen. At age sixteen. One person said age twenty-one, and everyone gasped. My face got hot. It was not like me to get anxious when asked a question, but when someone jovially turned the conversation to me, I lied. "I was so young. Like thirteen. I don't even remember it, but it was so awkward."

From there, I took control. "Justin, do you remember yours? Or were you old enough to really remember?" I knew Justin was a storyteller, and off he went. I laughed extra loud and hid behind the other stories.

That was the first time in life when I'd felt old and behind. Until then, I had done a miraculous job of feeling set apart, out of the game. And it worked. If you're not a gymnast, there's no reason to feel insecure about your double-back-handspring-into-a-triple-twist. Simone Biles can do it, and good for her. But you're not competing with her, so who cares? Maybe you can watch a gymnastics tournament and yell at the TV and have all kinds of opinions. This is how I felt about romance. My friends were torn up about boyfriends and girlfriends, this relationship imploding while that one was on fire. I'd become a go-to for processing and advice while leaving myself completely out of it.

In the years since, I'd been busy. New friends. Spiritual awakenings. A dream job at a nonprofit I believed in. And lucky for me, I wasn't walking around looking like a Hemsworth. I was cute but not beautiful, so straight girls and gay boys weren't crashing their cars into mine for attention. I was funny, and on top of that, oblivious. So deeply entrenched in the Christian world that I didn't know any openly gay people. Or maybe I knew a few, but they were on the periphery. To pursue friendship with them would mean exposing myself to undue temptation and risking my role as the token gay character in a group of straight friends. Self-hatred can walk around disguised as successful assimilation.

Through it all, I had simply never noticed that I'd reached my late twenties without ever kissing anyone. Until I noticed. And then I felt deeply lacking. Embarrassed. Less than human. I spent the rest of that Uganda trip wondering if I'd missed my chance. If I was too far behind to be fully human. Somewhere deep in my mind, I was taking apart the things that had kept me unkissed. I was closing the Bible. I was plugging my ears. I was trying to think for myself.

As I rode the train south with Osama's dead body on everyone's lips, I thought, "Who is going to pick me up this late?" Then I did the thing that so many before me have done. I thought, "Maybe this guy will inconvenience himself for me. If he really does have a crush on me, he'll pick me up."

He quickly said yes. I remember thinking, "Whoa, that's cool. Am I . . . am I in the game?"

The train pulled into the station around ten-thirty, and there he was. Wearing a maroon T-shirt and khaki shorts that showed his strong legs. His blond hair perfectly curled up like a wave. He'd even parked his car and met me *inside* the station, a highly unnecessary and deeply chivalrous move.

We walked to his car, where he had a bottle of red wine in a paper bag on the front seat. "So there is this little beach facing Coronado, in the bay, no one knows about it. I'm taking you there," he said, smiling mischievously.

"Oh, wow, I thought I'd explored all of San Diego. I have no idea where you're talking about." I exaggerated my ignorance to make him feel extra knowledgeable. "I am stoked about this wine," I said, grabbing his shoulder with a sustained hold. "'Goodbye Osama' deserves a drink!" This, as many of you will know, is called flirting.

Most people begin flirting very young, and practice it in their early teens. It is play fighting. Conscious and subcon-

scious touching. You act insulted by their every move, testing them, I guess, forcing them to protest and say that they
didn't mean it, that they really care about you. The language
of flirtation is indirect. Plausible deniability. This works well
for closeted gay boys. They can flirt and call it friendship.

Even in my asexual youth, I did this. I did it with lots of
straight boys, and they did it back. I lived in the broad undefined sexual limbo of male friendship—a soup of joking,
wrestling, and deep affection through Christian intimacy
and spiritual deep-talks. Something sexual was always humming in the ether, though calling it "sexual" feels like a betrayal. It was just magnetism, not entirely sexual but
somehow related.

I fell in love with my straight best friends a few times.
Once in high school. Once in college. And once after. This
love masked itself in me as best-friendship. As being insepa-
rable. As writing what can only be described as love notes to
each other, and always speaking about the friendship itself,
how extraordinary it was. I didn't recognize it as love. But it
was. They could spend every minute with me, endless
sleepovers and hugs and talks 'til sunrise. They could love
me in every way except with their skin. But this unrequited
love, however well justified in my head, stored up in my
heart like enriched uranium. An explosive *not-having*. A
longing for completion that vibrated through my whole
body.

The feeling was invisible to me, until I got into that car
with Jackson.

On the drive, we flirted, openly. Touching hands to knees.
Laughing at everything. And the potential end of this flirting

was full embrace. Sexual touch. I felt it coming, the biological end-purpose of flirting. For the first time in my life, I was playing the game of nature. Though the goal of that biological game—procreation—is unlikely, the programming remains.

We turned onto a random side street behind a strip mall, then parked on a residential street. The houses were nice, as are all houses in coastal San Diego. There was a little path between them, almost invisible through the trees. We walked down it and ended up on a sandy beach. A small crescent of sand behind the houses. The water of the bay was still, like a lake, and the lights of downtown San Diego shimmered across it. Jackson had a blanket under his arm and wine in his other hand. He picked a spot and laid the blanket down. I opened the twist-cap wine. We sat down and drank from the bottle.

To be honest, I don't remember what we talked about. Maybe Osama bin Laden. Maybe the music we were listening to, or our weekend activities. I do remember how easily I slipped into being pursued. He touched my knee. I let him. I laughed and shuffled closer at his jokes. We drank the wine. Everything was funny. Somehow his leg was thrown over mine. I pulled it closer. I let it thread my legs.

We were there, talking about nothing, when he leaned in and kissed me. I will be very forensic about this. He lightly bit my lower lip. He didn't rush in with the tongue. He pulled me in with his right hand while holding himself up with his left. He didn't know it was my first time.

I was in the kiss, and at the same time floating above it. This is not an unusual experience, especially during a big moment like sex or graduation or a wedding. We are watching ourselves do the thing as we do the thing. We are wondering how we look. But there is an added lucidity to it when it happens at age twenty-eight. I wasn't a teenager, disgusted by my changing body, intoxicated by my hormones, clumsy in my newness on the earth. I was an adult man. I knew who I was and even liked myself. I knew how to live and make money and make friends. All these other confusions weren't swarming in the mix. They were more or less settled. So this newness, this discovery, was crystallized in its isolation.

For transparency's sake, it wasn't exactly my first time. I had kissed a girl, Natalie, during my sophomore year of college. She heard that I hadn't kissed anyone, and announced in the sushi restaurant that she would teach me. She was sitting next to her boyfriend, who knew very well that I was her gay sidekick. She scooted close to me and gave me instructions. "Keep your lips soft but firm. Don't use your tongue too much but you can a little. Don't bang your teeth, but don't stay too far away." None of these rules made any sense. We gave it a try.

"Okay, okay . . . less like eating a sandwich," she said. *Yikes.* I tried again, and I can't tell if I got better or she gave up.

That was the first and last time my lips had touched lips. And I never counted it as my first kiss because that seems to require some level of attraction. Right? Not cold education, but hunger.

As Jackson kissed me, I wondered if I was okay at it. One thing I could tell: He was liking it. He now had me on my back and we were squirming. Legs braiding. My mind was busy: *Is this making out? This feels really nice. Wow, the mouth-on-mouth contact is so intimate. Now I understand why Julia Roberts wouldn't kiss any of the men in* Pretty Woman. *Wow, having someone's weight on you is sexy. Oh no, our teeth hit. Okay, control the teeth, Jed. Wow, his mouth tastes like a mouth, gamy or something, which should be gross, but I'm into it. I'm very into it.*

We kissed and made out for however long. It was a wholly positive experience. Maybe it approached midnight or later and it was time to go. I had work the next day. We got back in his car and held hands. We laughed a lot. We kissed again as I got out of the car at my house.

I wanted more kisses. I felt accomplished, more human, no longer as incomplete. I was still two years away from having sex for the first time, but now I was on the train track. And as much as I'd glorified shucking the assembly line of life—doing my own thing and not fitting in—all I'd ever wanted to do was belong. To be human in the most fundamental way. The accoutrements could be rebellious, but the bones needed to be solid. Even ordinary. I wanted to be in love and have a husband and maybe a family.

I have, in the years since that kiss, played the game that everyone else is always playing. I've dated. I've struggled to understand my faith's fraught relationship with body and desire. I've peeled away shame like healing sunburnt skin. I've had a few boyfriends. I've released a hell of a lot of oxytocin. I've flirted and made out and had some sex. Not a ton, but some. I still feel very green. At thirty-seven, I do this little equation in my head all the time: Most people start dating at seventeen, or have sex around then. So if I started at thirty, that means I'm romantically twenty-four. Maybe it's not bad that I'm still figuring this all out.

THE LONGING TO find someone is one of life's most fundamental feelings. Our music celebrates or vilifies it. Our movies and TV shows, too. Our long talks with friends so often revolve around it.

Love is hard. We expect our romantic partners to be our best friends, the objects of our desire, the home we return to, and the adventure we seek. We want to lust for them like strangers but trust them like family. We want to keep some mystery, but begrudge them if they keep secrets. We want them to be an entire community in one. To be every member of the village. When they can't satisfy all of those needs—and of course they can't—our eyes and thoughts stray as we wonder if we've made a mistake.

We expect to know our soul mates when we see them, without question, like Rachel McAdams grinning under Spanish moss. Any doubt, any testing, throws the fantasy into disarray. We've combined Western individualism with the ancient institution of marriage. It is no longer a contract to ensure the safety of life and family in a hostile world. It is now supposed to be the miraculous meeting of two independent souls who complement each other in perfect harmony.

How, then, do we proceed? How do we find and keep love? Is it even possible?

ASK ME WHAT it's like to be in love, and I will say, "Have you ever been in love?" If you tell me no, I will try to use a metaphor, but it won't work. If you ask me, "Do you know what it's like to lose your mother?" I will say, "No, but I did lose my grandmother." And you will say, "No, it is not like that." If I ask you, "Is being a mother everything you thought?" you will say, "No, it's more. I can't explain it."

The truest things are unteachable. I can study a map of Patagonia for a hundred years and know a hell of a lot about it. I can wow people at cocktail parties with my knowledge. But then one woman strolls in who has been there, stood there, felt there, and I am a buffoon. A map is helpful, of course. It can show you the way, and keep you safe. But it must be used in tandem with the going. Words are maps to human experience. Helpful, full of tips and tricks. But life must be lived for the words to make sense. The most beautiful or heartbreaking things (which are often so near to each other) can only be felt.

It makes me wonder why we force kids to read the classics. I read Steinbeck in eighth grade. I hated it.

In my life, I've seen a thousand photos of an eclipse. So have you. But actually standing beneath one, feeling one, having the world go dark in the middle of the day, screaming with your friends and imagining ancient people losing their shit over the insanity, the godliness of it . . . Words are garbage, until you've seen the thing they describe. Then words are a way to spread it around to your fellow witnesses, to keep the feeling going.

Words are meant for the living.

If you love someone, you must learn to speak their language. If your words do not mean the same thing, you'll end up talking at them and resenting them for not understanding you. Seek first to listen, and learn the meaning of their words.

. . .

I WENT TO a beautiful wedding in Big Sur, and the whole experience reminded me of how different love is from friendship. I mean the love that leads to marriage. To commitment. It is concerned with the future, the promises, the excitement of all that lies ahead. Deep friendship is recognition that two people are already on the same journey with the same destination. It's a fun high five on the path. Love is that, too, but also the knowledge that the other person *is* the journey. That the other person is part of your life's big commission. Partnership. At the same time, there is no real loss of self. There is always autonomy. It is a paradox between separateness and oneness.

I remember having a chat with Ruthie one time about all this.

"I think I could be single forever," I said. "I don't need another person to feel whole. I like who I am single."

"Of course you do," she said. "We all do, because then we can live in perfect selfishness. We can bounce and leave whenever we want. We can ghost. We can ignore or move on a whim. When you commit your heart to another, you learn about your selfishness, your laziness, your quirks and idiosyncrasies that are invisible to you on your own. You miss a whole half of who you are when you don't bare your underbelly to the heart of another. And of course that is scary, but that's what falling in love is for. . . . It overrides your fear, and you just do it, whether you want to or not."

Welp. That was damning. And true. It's one thing to be happy alone, whole in yourself. To be open to love but happy without it. It's another to reject love because of fear. To choose safety over the bigness of risking your heart.

THE HEART AND the head. I obsess over their disagreements. They misunderstand each other. Or ignore each other. And the barrage of mixed signals from one to the other is the root of anxiety.

Take heartbreak, for example. How funny that the head knows the heart, knows how it feels and why, but the heart cannot hear the head. It is one-way communication. You know the path forward, you know you will feel better with time, you know that timing is God, and that somewhere down the road you'll be thankful for it all, and amused at how much you'd thought you lost. You know it all—but each feeling hits you fresh, as if the heart had no premonition or warning. As if it's not listening to you.

Because it's not.

The heart cannot hear. It bangs through a dark kitchen, burning its hands on everything and swearing it smells something good. It must learn. And it does. But only through experience and over time.

And yes, sometimes the heart was right all along. That's the rub.

I CAN DO something, know it's wrong, beat myself up for it, and keep doing it, helpless. This is not rare.

A friend of mine is having trouble with a new relationship. "I have tried to sabotage this thing at every turn," he said. "She is kind to me, loving and patient. She knows I haven't dated much and that I have intimacy issues."

He gulped down his cocktail and kept spilling his guts.

"She is so patient with me and my shit. It took me months before I admitted to myself that I really liked her. She was taking that wall down, brick by brick, and it worked. I finally feel like I'm present with her. Just enjoying her. Not freaking out.

"But man, the last few months were torture, because I knew I was blowing something good. I couldn't help myself. I would send her away and then lie in bed all night and ask myself, 'What the hell is wrong with me?'"

How devilish is the division of our mind and our motivations. It's like we watch ourselves, from behind soundproof glass, and our bodies act out a horror show before us.

I think a lot of people are living in fortresses. Built from wounds and the mess of growing up complex in a world that oversimplifies us. I think the work of adulthood is taking down walls, and allowing people with big and patient love to take them down for us. But, sheesh, if the walls are down, where is your defense? What about the little boy in middle school, scared of the big watching world?

I suppose that's where we choose adulthood, choose the harder way, choose strength.

THE MADNESS OF having a crush. The checking to see if they've been tagged in new photos, if they're commenting on photos and whose photos. The Internet has turned anyone infected with infatuation into a private detective, a one-person Patriot Act surveillance team.

I remember once being on a plane, trapped without stimuli and feeling so in love with someone that I thought I would claw my eyes out by the time I landed. My mind was lost in a spiral of imagining his thoughts and actions as personal attacks on me. How hilarious to remember that now. It wasn't hilarious then.

What's most convicting is how selfish a crush is. It isn't an openhanded celebration of the other person. Of saying how wonderful they are and letting them be what they are without attachment. It has little to do with them and everything to do with you. Your value. Your ownership. Your success in seduction. They just happen to be the form your self-worth is possessing for the moment. Then, maybe they like you back, and the fire suddenly cools, and you wonder, "Wait, am I even ready for a relationship? Will my friends even like him? Do we have anything in common?"

Maybe this isn't so universal. Maybe I'm showing my cards. Whatever. I love reading my old journals and remembering the lunacy. Maybe I'll remember my laughter when this inevitably happens again.

THE FIRST PHASE of having a crush is treacherous. You like how someone looks, their tone and vibe, the way they dress. The items on your checklist are getting checked. Ooh, they said something funny? Check. They like black coffee and Rascal Flatts? This is looking GOOD. Right about then, somewhere between your eyes and stomach, the pheromones kick in and start pulling the levers of your brain, and this person becomes all you can think about.

This is when things can go wrong. Imagine you have a

long checklist of traits that you think make someone compatible. It's maybe fifty things if you're picky, or fifteen if you're not. Some of these things you could list off right now. Others are subconscious, preferences you don't know you have, and you know them only when you see them. Check, or *yikes*.

The trickiness of the crush is that your brain does something unfair in this moment. This dreamy human has checked off the first five on the list. Looking good, right? Then the brain just goes ahead and checks off everything else. Check check check check. Right then, they become fantasy. Could this person be the answer to my holy checklist? Could they?

And so, you create a fake person. You imagine someone who looks like your crush, sounds like your crush, but has all your checks checked. You want to date that person. But the person—the real person, I mean—keeps showing you who they are. And suddenly, check number forty-seven gets X-ed out. Then twenty-four. One after another. And you resent your boyfriend or girlfriend for not being the person your imagination created them to be.

Maybe you settle, stick around. Still, you are hurt and angry and in knots at the tiny deaths of your fantasy. In your resentment, you might not see that a lot of your checklist was unnecessary or misguided. And when you feel that knotting, you take it out on this poor person who never promised to be anyone but who they really are.

Chances are, they did this to you, too.

COUPLES WANT THE romance to last. They say they don't want to lose the spark. What they mean is the electric sense of mystery that was present in the beginning. "Romance" was the journey from crush to relationship, when you wondered if the other person was the fulfillment of your desires and needs, and for a time they were. Every exchange, every dinner, every kiss was charged with these questions. Charged with "What if they are everything I ever wanted, and what if they are more than I could have imagined?!" The exhilaration is rooted in the wondering, in the hopeful uncertainty. It is the questions that give it energy, not the answers.

Of course, this type of wondering isn't sustainable, nor should it be.

Travel is the same. I want seduction. Perhaps the new place will give me what I need, answer my questions, wake me up, free me. The romance of travel is the hope of what it can teach me, show me. And just like love, it makes me feel completely, frantically alive.

But there is a time for the thirst of romance, and there is a time for building a home. You realize that the street you live on is overflowing with wonders. The world is a teacher, not only because it is new, but because it is both yours and never completely yours. And ever changing.

In time, romance and commitment become one thing. An inhale and an exhale. I hope to live my sunset years nestled in this understanding.

WHY DOES SOMETHING have to last forever to be right? Why can't you move to a foreign city and kiss some randoms and rent a flat and then come back and start again? Why can't you fall in love and discover it wasn't right and move on while thanking the relationship for what it was? Love doesn't seem to allow this, because it trades in absolutes. In forevers. That is what falling in love is, the endless planning and dreaming, the holding of the beloved with the pulsing hope that this holding will extend beyond the horizon.

I don't think you can fall in love and know for sure that it is temporary. That isn't love. That is sex and fun and friendship. But I do think you can fall in love with the sober wisdom that humans change and factors arise that are beyond the calculations of anyone . . . and if that happens, it isn't the end of the world. It is the real world. There doesn't have to be a villain for someone to get hurt.

As I get older and listen to my life, the truest things seem to live in paradoxical tension. Hope holding hands with understanding. Expectation dancing with the hard lessons of humility. The human heart piloting the mystery of the human heart.

NOTHING IS SO cold as desire unfulfilled. You want something or someone so bad, and your mind works at it like a cancer, eating at you until you don't recognize yourself. We have all been in this place. But real life is wise, and denies you things from time to time. Wisdom is not gentle, but it is kind, because it knows the real world is where peace lives. It knows that the happiness of fulfilled desire is as lasting as the first bite of cake.

MY FRIEND ELIZABETH asked me a tough question: "If all your exes were asked to describe you in one word, what word would they agree on?"

I don't have enough exes to form some sort of chorus, but my guess would be "self-forgiving." I am such a student of living, so interested in my own nature and the lessons to be learned from my mistakes, that I think I may forgive myself too quickly. I say to myself, "Jed, you didn't know better until now. Now you know. Good on you." All the while, I may have hurt someone.

I don't know if I really understand the words "should have." This is a common characteristic of fast-talkers. We can sew a silver story around anything we do, and leave people spinning under a spell. Leave them hurt and feeling dumb for feeling hurt and without the words to defend their position.

I want to grow, to do right by others and myself, to trust the open doors and knock on the closed ones. But I sometimes get scared of my own mind. Of my words. Of my ability to forgive myself. Of my self-assuredness. I need to let myself feel confusion. I need to be embarrassed once in a while. I need to cry and feel and know that I can't explain it all away. I need the powerlessness of fog.

I'm leaning into the middle place, the unknowing, the place I don't control.

THE FIRST BOY I ever had a crush on was in the eighth grade. I mean, we both were. I'll call him Charlie. At the time, I was soft and pale and covered in acne. I swam with my shirt on. I had no knees, just white tubes for legs.

Charlie was cool. He had a six-pack. He was tan and funny. He spoke like an adult. He broke rules. And he was nice to me. Maybe he was patronizing me, or even snickering behind my back to his cool friends. But at that age, the fact that his godlike face even looked at me, knew my name . . . it felt good. The hormones and confusion transformed him into something more than a person. He became an icon of desire.

But it wasn't just desire. It was envy. I don't know if this is something straight people experience, but when you're attracted to the same sex, there is another layer mixed in. Not only do I desire the person, but I compare myself to them. Their body. Their hair. Their face. I long for it, and am jealous of it. Or feel shame for my inadequacy. The natural otherness of heterosexuality may insulate most people from this feeling. But for me, it was just another charge in the electric chaos of my feelings.

Middle school, man. Those years. When the innocence and isolation of childhood are plugged into the circuit board of the world, of comparison and longing, and all that electricity comes flowing in like a flood in a canyon . . . and we all get fried.

"NEVER GO TO bed angry." I've heard that said at so many wedding toasts. I'm sure it's mostly true, but my brain doesn't work like that. I get emotional or upset, and when I go to bed, the quiet darkness of my dreaming calms the growling wolf. I wake up the next day feeling much better. The thing that stirred me up feels smaller, or at least my reason gets a go at it apart from my hot chest and feelings. Sleep does wonders.

I'm an external processor and an optimist. My words are tests. They leap out from me, and I watch how they land.

That's how I discover what I think and feel. I have friends who process in their heads. I'm not sure if they are thinking in silent sentences, but they seem to consider all the roads before they pick one. I'm sure that's a better way to be. I rarely ask for directions. But I thank God for sleep. I don't think well when I'm awake. I just talk. But when I sleep, I rise with new understanding, as if wisdom entered into my ears like a dust storm. In the morning, I can see. The dust has settled and the landscape is revealed before me.

I am not married and never have been. But when I've been worked up about something in my past relationships, talking about it has sent us deeper into the double-helix dance of misunderstanding. But a good night's sleep did some rearranging. I've woken up and forgotten why we were fighting at all.

I think this is why I've always loved the look of people sleeping. No matter how big, tough, rugged, fierce, or loud while awake, a sleeping person is innocent. Helpless and soft. Regal.

SOME PEOPLE ARE madly in love and wrong for each other. Magnets on fire. The sex is amazing and the fighting never ends. The contempt, the cutting remarks in front of friends. Or life circumstances that would never work. One person a nomad. The other, domestic. One wants kids, the other never.

To me, this is one of the most unfortunate burdens of having a human heart. You love each other. You come together with passion and connection so deep, it is certainly instinctual, from a million years ago. But your ego, the rational part of you, picks at the other person. Cuts them down. They cut you down, and you pout to force their hand. You would die for them—and they just might kill you—but your chemistry is a puppeteer, and losing them feels like death. The moment the loss happens, you feel as if you have misplaced the best thing in your life. You forget the fighting and misery. The wise counsel of your friends is a foreign language, the murmurings of a Charlie Brown adult. You are driven by a mystery that turns the ship without your consent.

This is a great sadness of being human. We are both an ancient monkey and a supercomputer. They often don't get along. Desires and instincts misaligning in pain. This happens in love, career, family, so many things.

So little of life is rational. But I will say this: When the chemicals drain from the brain, and a moment's rest gives your thoughts some clarity, there comes a time when you can bandage the wounds and prepare for the next hurricane. At least you'll know you aren't crazy. You're human. And everyone knows the feeling.

WEDDINGS ARE ONE of the few traditions in our culture with a structure that we mostly adhere to. And a lot of us point our lives toward that event, setting it in our own stories as a pinnacle, a goal, a mile marker of achievement. This can cause a lot of idolatry and grief and impossible expectations. I've been to a lot of incredible weddings. Beautiful celebrations of commitment. But they can blur together, and feel performed rather than experienced. The feeling of,

"Okay, we're supposed to say this now, and now this." Vendors inflating fees. Stuffy clothes choking laughter. Fantasies dashed on the hardness of reality.

Well, I just felt something new. I went to the best wedding yet. Because the people getting married morphed the ceremony, honed it, changed it to feel fresh and honest. It wasn't in a church or a building; it was in a grove of redwoods. We dressed in costumes. White and gold. I wore tights and spray-painted my white jacket gold. Face paint everywhere. The decorations were hung by friends. Everyone camped in tents and tipis by the river.

For the ceremony, the local college marching band led us in a celebratory march through a persimmon grove. The bride and groom read vows that expressed the honest surprise that a partner could be found in this life, a comrade. They didn't pretend they were perfect. They celebrated the shadow and the light, conscious that they were signing up for a lifetime of self-discovery. We danced until four A.M. under the unpolluted bright stars of rural Northern California. The whole thing made me feel as if marriage had just been invented, a brilliant new idea.

That night, I didn't feel the sting of comparison, of, "Wow, I hope I find this one day." I was too wrapped up in the awe that such a thing could exist at all. That something so pure is a gift not to the couple alone, but to the community.

Love is real. It's built in communities and orchards and the acts of working together and standing together. I was glowing that week as if a mirror could hold on to sunshine and reflect it around for days.

. . .

I ONCE READ that babies see the world upside down for the first few days after they're born. The eye actually projects the world that way onto your retinas, and it takes the brain a little while to learn to flip it over. Your brain is doing that right now, flipping the world to appear as if it's standing right-side up.

I heard someone describe falling in love as being turned upside down. Whatever your brain had learned—that up is up and down is down—it changes. Your priorities are thrown in disarray. You don't sleep. You don't eat the same. You feel drugged. You are newly born.

It happens outside of love, too. A conversation can be so mind-altering that I'll feel turned over for a minute. A new perspective or a loving challenge will cause me to rethink myself. And I must learn to see this new world right-side up. It seems like life wants me to turn over my house sometimes and see what sticks to the floor.

IF YOU WENT to college and now live in a big city, you will probably be single longer than your parents were. People are getting married later, having kids later. Especially the urban and the educated. The traditional time frame for starting a family has moved back a decade. So on one hand, being single has never been more okay. Spending time finding yourself, building your career, has never been more socially sanctioned. But the tension still lives. We may not feel anxious about being single at twenty-four, but we do at thirty-four. Many of my successful single lady friends have spent big money freezing their eggs. The finite window of fertility doesn't care about you finding "the one."

But it doesn't have to be about the limited life of eggs or safe pregnancy. It can be about your own life, about wanting love in your most able years, about the firework mythology of love. We want that big love. We want to be surprised by our "person." We want the story to be worth telling and cooing about. We spend all this time building our best selves, and it makes us demand someone who has also done the same. Sixty years ago, you married someone who was good enough. Over 50 percent of those marriages ended in divorce. But I don't think that's because they weren't proper soul mates. I think it's because the expectation of being with your soul mate became our dominant cultural expectation, so being in those marriages felt like a mistake. They got divorced and jumped into the river of big hopes for love.

This is the tightrope I've found myself walking. Accepting that being single is okay, that I am happy with who I am, and if it's meant to be it'll happen. But seek and you shall find. The person of your dreams isn't going to find you on the couch.

I've heard stories of total life pivots coming from a chance encounter, a risky new job, a last-ditch effort to try something new, a rock-bottom whim. We've been attracted to the wrong people for the wrong reasons, seeking their affection or their bodies or their coolness to heal insecurities from middle school, self-hatred that thinks it can be erased by kissing the thing that hurt it. We've wanted a specific career, but when we achieve it, we find it empty of meaning. We've wanted marriage to escape loneliness and ridicule, only to end up lonelier in a marriage with a shiny fake smile.

We think we know how things should be and how they will arrive.

We don't know what's coming in our lives. We are like those doomsday pastors who predict the day and time of Christ's return, only to shrink in embarrassment when the predictions are wrong.

There are two schools of thought at war with each other. One tells you to manifest your dreams. The other, to surrender to the universe. I hear both, talking to me from either shoulder.

So, what do we do? Well, I'm currently being torn limb from limb, dating and looking for the right one. Wondering if this guy is gonna be it, or fade away. Or if that other guy, the one I was really excited about who wasn't excited back, will ever circle back around. I don't know. But I can feel an answer in there somewhere. It has something to do with holding the paradox in your hands. Playing with it, as the universe often invites us to do. Most things of real meaning are the humming tension between two opposites. Marriage, for example: loving commitment to another autonomous soul. Becoming one, and yet clearly separate. Sexual wanting, and safe having. Adventure, yet home. In the constant re-upping. In the flow of change and decision.

I think God asks us to tango with it.

To try things with gusto. To understand that we are ignorant actors in a cosmic drama. To believe we deserve things, knowing that we might be taught something surprising in our entitlement. To want with all our might, knowing that our wanting might be misguided. To risk the embarrassment of asking, and to receive whatever the answer is. To walk in faith, not sit in faith. To move away from home, because we must go out on our own, but to know deep down, if it all goes to shit, we can always move back in with Mom.

I LEARNED A new word when I was in Brazil: *saudade*. It is Portuguese and pronounced something like "sow-dajeh."

The word doesn't have a direct translation in English. It describes a deep, heavy longing, a nostalgia, a melancholic ache for an absent something or someone you love. It brings the happiness and sadness of love and longing together. It captures the hole in your sternum and stomach that knots and swells and can be filled by only one person or place. It often carries the sad subtext of knowing that the object of your love may never return. It pains you, and yet, some quality of it feels good. It is both terrible and beautiful. You can even feel *saudade* for someone who is presently with you, because you feel their future loss, even as you are with them now.

For me, *saudade* captures those blessed horrible seconds when you become aware of a perfect moment, and feel it dripping through time never to return again. Suddenly you're watching it from outside your body, and your heart cries to cast it in iron and hold it forever.

I wondered if English had words that Portuguese doesn't. I read online that Portuguese has *saudade,* but doesn't have "atonement." How interesting. That the English have a word for paying for your sins, and the Brazilians have a word to celebrate the heartache of missing someone.

· · ·

I WAS HAVING dinner with Ruthie awhile back, and we fell into one of our late-night, red wine couch conversations. We circled around the idea that you can't love others if you don't love yourself. That it isn't selfish to love yourself, because true love can come only from abundance, not from lack. Everything else is the ego seeking affirmation and the sexual instinct seeking release.

I've dated guys who were simply my teenage self reaching back and getting what he never had. The jock I'd fantasized over in high school? I dated the equivalent of him as a twentysomething. The chic cool kid? He was next. The hot business guy? Next. As if I was making up for lost time. My attractions were almost entirely formed by my old embarrassments, my old lusts. My body wanted what it had been denied in the years when my sexuality turned on. I knew these guys were wrong. I knew our lives didn't mesh or match. But my attraction was driving my insecurities and lacks.

If you are motivated by insecurity and self-hatred or embarrassment, you will use your relationships to heal those wounds. You'll look to attention, attraction, and distraction as a way to fix yourself. You are always aware of how you're coming across, dragging behind you the fear of being left out, forgotten, or found annoying. You are often offended.

Ruthie and I talked about how the most loving people we know are so comfortable in their own skin that the attention they give and love they share is totally free of expectations and baited traps. These people rarely get their feelings hurt, because they aren't worried how they're coming across or how they're being treated. They're too busy being interested in everyone and everything else. I don't know how to help someone love themselves, but if we stopped treating one another as a means to an end but rather as the end itself, I think it would help.

Maybe that's the key to it all: You are an end in and of itself. And so is your beloved. I have yet to prove this to myself, but I've seen it, and I believe it.

Work

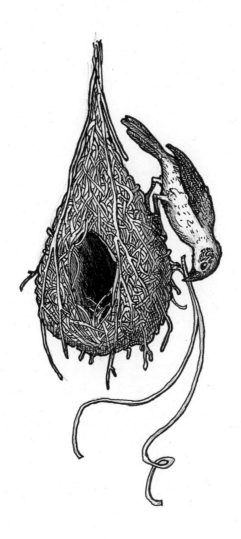

A touch of perspective. We've been anatomically human for about 300,000 years. We've had specialized jobs for about 5,000 to 10,000 of those years. Which means, for the vast majority of the history of our species, this modern problem of finding a calling or ho-humming about not liking your job didn't exist. There was no such thing as a career. You hunted. You gathered. You raised babies and made a shelter. That's it. It sounds so wild and different than the life you currently know, but it wasn't that long ago. Even as recently as a couple hundred years ago, most of us would have been farmers. Maybe you complained about it, but never with the illusion that you could find some other way of life. Our modern-day existential identity crisis is only about two or three grandmas old.

Okay. Now that we have some perspective, let's stress out about finding your calling in the modern age.

I WENT TO law school. The majority of people go there for two reasons: to have a job that makes a lot of money, or to have a job that impresses people. I met only a few who loved justice.

My own motivations were foggy. I studied poetry and creative writing in undergrad and worried I'd never earn a dollar. I wanted a proper skill that could make money. I was evangelical Christian at the time and I wanted to fight for the oppressed. I wanted to learn human rights law and rescue slaves. I also wanted to be an entertainment lawyer, and represent James Cameron or something in a massive contract negotiation. Or I wanted to write screenplays and be able to negotiate my own contracts. I liked the idea of having a law degree. It felt bougie and legitimate.

Law school was about $150,000, on top of an undergrad bill that was roughly the same size. I had tremendous financial aid because my single mom made almost no money. But I knew a few people who took loans for both and finished law school $300,000 in debt. From there, they needed to land good law jobs. And the law jobs that pay the best are the ones that are least "fun" to do. The furthest from the courtroom dramas we've grown up watching on television. Endless paperwork. Working hundred-hour weeks as an associate, making good money, but doing so at the cost of your sanity and the sight of sunlight. You promise yourself you'll pay off your loans and then make some money and get a different job. Maybe you'll start your own firm or find a less stressful place to work. As soon as you get out of debt, you'll live the life you want.

Instead, here's what happens: The money's so good that you can't just live humbly and pay off all that debt. You need to blow off steam. You need a nice car and dope clothes. You need to date and fall in love. (Sex is a nice release.) So you find someone good and get engaged. Now you're buying them nice things to impress them with your paycheck. Now you're married, and she's pregnant. You need a house. And you're on your way to making partner at the firm. "Wait, I didn't want partner," you think. "I'm just trying to get out of debt." You're making decent payments on those loans, but not giant ones, because now you have a car payment and a house payment and a lifestyle. Now you've got kids and they are expensive. You're now junior partner. Where did eight years go?

You're in deep now. If you leave, you'll lose all that seniority, all that progress, all that proximity to big, big money. "Okay," you think. "When I make partner, I'll be able to be fully debt free and rich." But now your kids are in high school. They need cars, and maybe you want to send them to a private school. You never saw yourself as a "lawyer," but now you're in your forties. This is the life you're living. Your one and only life. You wake up at sixty and wonder: Did I choose my life, or did I just pay bills and buy things to make paying bills less dreary?

This cascade of life choices, or siloing of options, all stemming from such early causes, happens to so many people. This picture of life scared me.

There is a bizarre tension in the model we're given: Adults tell us to find a job that fulfills our passion, but chances are you won't know your passion young enough, so the pressure of growing up and the passing of time will push you toward a conventional job. If you want a job that brings esteem, it will cost you a lot of money to earn a degree. Then you'll be shackled to the debt you've acquired, limiting your ability to find or pursue that mystery passion. Or, if you don't get an expensive degree, you might take a less lucrative job while other things happen . . . like marriage and kids. The flexibility of youth gets complicated by the compounding of responsibilities and roles. We must know our passion early, or miss the magic window. When that happens, we enter the eternal cloud of what-ifs and disappointment.

. . .

WE ALL WANT freedom, and we think that means the ability to do what we want when we want, have what we want, and achieve what we want. But what if what we want is wrong? What if our desires are the result of middle school insecurities, childhood rejections, vanity, and unconscious lust?

That question always sends me into a spin. What if I am an outdoorsman because I was picked on for being girly as a kid? What if my lawyer friends are lawyers because they grew up poor and were ashamed of it? What if a cop became a cop because he felt powerless in seventh grade? What if an aid worker cannot face her inner pain, so instead she heals the world?

Not that any of these motivations are wrong. Indeed, many things we want come from a beautiful and clear place. But I think there's wisdom in that question. Maybe that's why so many people achieve the thing they've desired for years and immediately find it unfulfilling. The idol turned out to be just a shiny stone.

As I NAVIGATED picking a college major, thinking first I'd be a movie director, then not knowing, I believed that my job must complete me. "What do you want to be when you grow up?" had set itself up as the floor of my identity, and I was looking to find my calling, a job that would be my vocational soul mate. I recently read an article about "workism" in *The Atlantic,* and it framed some of the unrest I've always had around vocation and meaning.

The author, Derek Thompson, explains that workism is

the belief that vocation gives life meaning. Like a religion. We are religious apes, and we look for ethereal meaning to motivate our lives. Two hundred and fifty years ago, you did what your parents did and you found meaning in God, in God's mysterious plan, in the afterlife, in conversion or virtue. Then, in the twentieth century, came the concept of a "career," of climbing the ladder, of reaching VP after starting in the mail room. As the workplace evolved, Thompson says, the corporate ladder was no longer the goal. It is now finding your calling. Work that satiates your spiritual appetite. We believe you shouldn't stop looking until you've found it.

For a million years, work felt productive because its meaning was obvious. Food collection. Rearing children. Damming a stream. You put in effort and you saw a result. The product of your labor either fed you or protected you. But as work became specialized, and money became the most common religion in the world—a collective belief that paper or gold has the power to move people—the direct feeling of work-into-product disintegrated for millions of people. We shuffle papers and aim for quotas . . . for what? To not get fired. To make more paper. This has left a vacuum in our need for purpose and meaning.

In the modern world, politics is a sort of religion. We organize around sacred principles like border security or social justice. We develop blasphemy laws ("Don't question the Second Amendment" or "Don't question intersectionality"), and spend our collective energy deciding who is in the group and who is to be kicked out. Who is a "real American" or a "real ally"? Purity is important to sanctimonious apes.

Having grown up Christian, I spent my childhood hearing, "For those who love God, all things work together for good." The belief that real meaning lies in following God's plan, in loving others in Jesus's name. Who cares what your job is? Your real job is to be a child of God.

This is the ultimate salve of believing in God. A glaze over the rough edges of life, a promise that no matter how insane it gets, it will all work out. God is in control. Take that away, and what are people left with? Finding their passion in order to find their meaning. Their vocational soul mate. Marching in the streets for a different president. Sheltering dogs. We can't escape from our spiritual appetite for meaning.

I speak about this from a privileged place: I have found a job that fulfills me. I am the writer I hoped to become. I have my vocational soul mate. I am a secular dream. Yet here I am, critiquing the idea that our job must complete us. I don't know if it's good for everyone to look for it. I don't know if our job should be the source of our self-regard.

In high school, friends would say, "I just want to get married and be a mom." I thought, "That's it? That feels so antiquated and small." But now I think that it's every bit as meaningful as anything else. And more directly so. You work all day for the betterment of a child you can see. You can appreciate if they are well fed and happy, or if they're not. How is that any less admirable than being CEO of a start-up?

As religious belief wanes and dilutes and thins in America, can our jobs fill the void?

For me, I'd say life itself is meant to be our soul mate. The unfolding lessons. The plans we make and the surprises that change them. Our jobs and relationships and activism and entertainment are all meant to instruct us, or at least entertain our consciousness. This is the meaning. To grow and learn and delight in good things and rail against bad things and then tell the story later.

WHAT WILL MY grandkids be like and think? What norms and ways of being will transform by then? I wonder about things I assume today, and how quickly the tides of thought can change. How I'll be an old curmudgeon worried about the runaway activism of the youth.

A couple of hundred years ago, if you said, "Dad, I don't want to be a farmer. I want to be true to myself and make art," your dad might go, "Where did you hear such nonsense? How will you eat? Human beings weren't made to make art. They're made to work the soil." Now millions of kids grow up and their parents say, "Be whatever you want to be. Follow your passion. It may be a bumpy road, but as long as you work hard and treat people right, you'll make it."

The world expanded its horizons, and so did we. We always had these many skills and talents in us. We just didn't know how to express them as a society.

I think in the years to come, gender and sexuality will work just this way. We won't hold rigid expectations for our children. They'll be free to express themselves as openly as we express our careers and talents. Science supports a broader gradient scale of sexuality and gender, with a strong majority at either end—male and female—but we have shoved the not-insignificant middle into a rigid binary. This minority matters.

If I went back in time and told my great-great grandfather that I would make a living off a social media tool where strangers can read my writing and see my pictures on tiny computers in their pockets, he'd look at me and grunt and say, "Get back to the field." He'd worry about me and society and "kids today." He'd probably go off and pray for my soul.

WHEN I HAVE kids, I think I'm going to insist on a gap year after high school. No, a gap *four* years. One year of travel, three years of work in a new city. The assembly line of school then college then work is not as instructive for life as I would want. The more people I talk to, the more I realize that the end of college was for them the same as it was for me. They felt ejected into the world like a loosed puppy in the woods. Howling for the safety of our leashes.

I imagine if I had seen a bit of the world, backpacked and lived poor as dirt at nineteen years old, and then worked in a new city as an intern or in some crappy job, things would have been different. If I had learned some skills first—learned to pay bills and be independent, learned how scary it is to make rent—and *then* gone to college, I think I would have paid closer attention to the miracle of learning, of institutions designed to prepare your mind for a productive life.

I remember meeting older students in college, people who had lived in the real world and then decided to go back to school. They seemed like a different breed. They sat in the front of the class. They asked questions. They took notes. I was in the back, looking out the window without a care in the world. A kid in the fourteenth grade, draining the world for my pleasure.

. . .

THE SKEPTIC IN my head says, "Yeah, follow your dreams, but we all know at least one talentless kid who moved to Los Angeles, hoping to become an actor or a pop singer. Not everybody should follow their dreams."

My friend Justin gave me some clarity on this. He said, "You must ask, 'What do you love? And what loves you back?'" Meaning, don't just sing at open mics or act in short films or write essays on Medium and then blame the deaf world for not understanding your "art." If you're not contributing something that people want and need, it will not be received.

My first book was about quitting my job and bicycling down the length of Latin America. It was about chasing my dream to be a writer. After it came out, some of the most common questions I got were: How do I find my passion? What if I don't know what it is? And if I do, how do I get the nerve to quit my job and chase it?

I don't know anyone else's life. But I can tell you what I did for myself.

First of all, I accepted that life is lived in seasons; it's not a single arrow that hits or misses some imaginary bull's-eye. The bull's-eyes we create in our youth are made with such limited information and are tainted by advertising. As I look back over my twenties, I see how each job taught me something indispensable for the next season. Law school taught me that I could read and comprehend patterns in history. Working at a nonprofit taught me that I could articulate complex ideas. And as I blindly collected tools in my twenties, I discovered what I loved and what I didn't. Then I tested what I loved against my determination to be excellent at it, and against the unflinching honesty of strangers, and saw if it loved me back.

For me, writing was the thing that loved me back.

I can almost trace my writing career back to one person, an acquaintance named Brian. I met him once on a trip to Colorado and we became Facebook friends. That's it.

I had started a blog. A journal that existed in public, with zero readers. But the thrill of it being online colored the way I wrote. It made me journal in such a way that I imagined a distant reader, and made efforts in clarity and explanation that I hadn't worried about while writing in a physical journal.

I posted the link to one of my entries on Facebook. It was some brain dump on faith and God and whatever else I was processing in my midtwenties. I wrote it reflecting on conversations I was having with my friends. I wanted them to read it, so I posted it. This guy Brian, who I didn't really know, read it and messaged me. He told me that I had put words to his thoughts. He told me how much it had helped him. He told me to keep writing.

That did something to me. It wasn't just my friends encouraging me. It wasn't my mom's wonderful biased love. It was a vague acquaintance who had better things to do, responding to my writing.

I kept writing and posting it to Facebook, and a few other acquaintances responded. They told me they really liked it. Then they sent the links to their friends. Then those friends sent it to other friends.

Soon, I had a few hundred people I didn't know reading what I wrote. Commenting to one another on Facebook, talking to one another. And that was fuel to keep going. That gave me the confidence to commit to writing a book. Even if it failed, I would have done it and been proud of the doing. My worst fear was denying the nag of an unfulfilled possibility, and then regretting the middle decades of my life. I'd rather fail and learn than taint my years with the question "What if?"

This is true of writing or opening a restaurant or building an app or starting a lawn-mowing business. If you make something good, it will spread. Word will pass from person to person. But first you have to actually make something, and put it where it can be consumed. If your friends *really* like it, they'll share it. If they don't, they won't. They'll give you neutered compliments like "Wow, you really did it! Everyone gives up, but you did it," or "I'm so proud of you for putting yourself out there!" This is them encouraging you. This is not them telling you what you made is good.

But if they actually like it, they'll share it. Then, others might respond. Friends of friends. Then, maybe, friends of friends of friends. If that starts happening, maybe you're on to something. Maybe the food you cook is excellent. It doesn't need your personal connections, your beauty, your money, your sweet friends. It needs only itself.

Here's the other thing: I quit calling it a "passion." That word is so aggressive. It implies that if you aren't burning for what you do, then you aren't living right. I don't want to burn—at least not all the time. I want to lean into the steady goodness of making good things. I like calling writing my "interest" or "the channel through which I sense myself and serve others." I don't know. I want to be gentler with my callings, my seasons, and let them flow into one another. Without the fallen leaves of autumn, spring would not have the soil to bring new life.

IT MAKES ME laugh when someone says, "Get real, if everyone quit their jobs and took off on an adventure, the world would collapse. Some people have to work!" It makes me laugh because those people aren't talking to me, they're talking to themselves. I believe in hard work. I have never suggested that everyone should shuck all their responsibilities and create a massive experience-based travel-orgy. I am not an idiot. I believe in the honor of a day's work and a day's pay. I believe that a complex society needs all its moving parts, and each part has importance.

But I also believe that society is broken in a lot of ways, and the only way for that to be recognized is for a few of us to step away and look at it from afar. Or maybe all of us, in one short season of life or another, should step away.

After the Great Depression, our country ran on an ethos that saw hard work as a virtue in and of itself. It was a response to years of fear about joblessness and destitution. It wasn't about having a sexy job that overpaid you to be lazy and famous; it was about the privilege of working and having the opportunity to provide for your family. That generation did well, and they promised themselves they would give their children the things they never had. A bigger house. A backyard. An education. College. A car. A dog. Trips to Disneyland. This has been the hope of many parents. The unintended side effect of success: They spoiled the children and infected them with entitlement.

But the pendulum always swings back, because history cannot abide excess. Nowadays, you see disenfranchised young people unable to find meaning in their work, because work itself no longer conveys meaning. I believe this is partly a good thing. This is the puzzle of modern living in the developed world.

So we're getting creative, and carving out time to travel is just one response to the unquiet spirit. Give us a minute to ride this pendulum back to the bottom. It might turn out to be a wrecking ball, but we're looking for balance.

THERE'S AN ESSAY by Wendell Berry called "Poetry and Marriage," where he talks about how the form of a poem—the restrictions and boundaries of those words—creates the art inside them. A poem is made beautiful by restrictions in word choice. How it paces language, lets phrases float and land on their own. How it fits the most meaning into the smallest space.

Our culture, informed by marketing and advertising, creates an ethos of limitless consumption-happiness: We must follow the whim of our desire. Always. Turn when the gut says turn. Commit to nothing. Gorge on your options. No breaks. All gas. But desire needs limitations. Unfettered wanting will drive you mad, and unrestricted getting will drive you to depression. Los Angeles is full of trust-fund burnouts, living reminders that limitless access to money not only doesn't bring happiness, it seems to repel it. How often have I gotten what I wanted, and found it much less satisfying than it seemed from a distance?

Berry says, "Form serves us best when it works as an

obstruction to baffle us and deflect our intended course. It may be that when we no longer know what to do, we have come to our real work, and when we no longer know which way to go, we have begun our real journey. The mind that is not baffled is not employed. The impeded stream is the one that sings."

WHAT DO YOU want for yourself? How do you spend your energy? What stresses you out? What is the "why" behind your toiling?

Make a list, a brutally honest list.

Do you want to make your parents proud? Do you want to have someone beside you, so you won't be alone? Do you want love because you'd be a good partner, or because you want to avoid the embarrassment you feel about being single? Do you want more friends? How many? Do you want a certain number of followers? Do you want fame? For what? To be famous for no reason? What is the unique thing you bring to the table? Why should they follow you? Do you want money? How much? Then what? Do you want to like yourself? Why should you? What do you do that is likable? Are you kind? Interested in others? Helpful? Or self-possessed in your self-hatred?

We think we want wealth, fame, and beauty. But we really want acceptance, community, and respect. So many of us chase the smoke when the fire is what we're really after. We buy fleeting clouds of smoke with money we sold our souls to earn.

. . .

WHAT IS CONTENTMENT? Being at peace with your life. What you have and earn and who you're with. Angry at nothing. It seems like it is the goal of the enlightened: to receive whatever life sends you without protest. To accept the flow of life and God and the universe. But what then of the agitation at your desk to change your life? Is discontent wrong?

I feel the pull of the window, calling me outside. Calling me to try other things. I also feel the Zen of acceptance, of making the best of the current season, of patience like a seed in the dirt. But when the spring rains come, those seeds sure get busy changing. That image of a seed waiting for rain— I wonder how many things in our lives fit in that metaphor. We get fired or offended or broken up with. We lose the job we wanted, or a bad president gets elected. One change we should accept. The other we should fight. How do I train myself to respond in the right season?

I am both content and fidgety. My hands are being pulled both east and west. If I can keep it just right, where it pulls but not too hard, it's a nice stretch. Like yoga.

I THINK OUR biggest tormentors in life are our expectations. I was supposed to be successful by now. I was supposed to have found true love by now. I was supposed to be loving my job by now. I should do life this way or that way because that's what I'm supposed to do, that's what people expect of me. I had hopes and dreams, and I used to think thirty was old. Now here I am, thirty-seven, feeling quite young.

.   .   .

IF YOU WANT to change something, the most important question you can ask yourself is: "To what end?" This is like casting a spell of reasonable thinking. If you are in a long-term relationship and long for casual sex with strangers, or to be single again just because it was autonomous and fun, imagine it. Imagine being single or having your casual sex. Then ask: To what end? To be back introducing yourself to randoms? To do the small talk? To feel the rush of a new body only to find them annoying the next day and want them out of your space?

If you wish you lived in a different city, to what end? If you don't like yourself here, chances are you won't like yourself in whatever place is occupying your daydreams. Do you want to be rooted or forever on the move? Do you want to leave home and travel the world for your life? To what end? To exchange deep community for sensation and thrill and an endless stream of acquaintances and skin-level conversations? Maybe you do! But it's good to interrogate the desire. Do you really want it, or are you just hungry or a little claustrophobic? Imagine having the thing you long for. Imagine having it for a long time. Will it wear off and return you to the twisted frustration you're in? Is your frustration honest or naïve?

Sometimes leaving your job and pursuing something new is the end you dreamed of. I know it was for me. But sometimes, it's just our human tendency to crave what we don't have. To never be satisfied.

I want to tease out that impulse. Listen to it when it's helpful and tame it when it's not. Ask the right questions that reveal my real motives. I want to be the type of person that takes risks I can be proud of. Not the ones that will feed me like junk food.

. . .

I HATE LEARNING new skills. It's embarrassing to try something and be terrible at it—especially as an adult, when I've begun to settle into "who I am" and "what I do." Learning is such work. And I like being praised for what I already know how to do.

But work leads to muscle memory, and muscle memory leads to art. I took piano lessons for eight years. I hated the lessons. I hated practicing fifteen minutes a day. I used to sit hunched over the piano as a little kid, doing the bare minimum of chords and arpeggios until the eternity of fifteen minutes had passed. I truly hated it.

Then, without noticing, years later, something happened to my fingers. They knew the chords. They moved over the keys without thought. I could think of a song I liked, and then my fingers would feel around the piano and figure it out. On their own.

I love watching experts move in their craft. Watching a chef command her kitchen, tearing through tickets and tables and orders and dishes in a flow of words and commands. Thoughtless as a waterfall. Perfect. Childhood moves slowly, I think, because we are in the clumsy process of work, of learning, of dragging ourselves to those piano lessons. Our mind is awake, learning how to turn effort into instinct.

When I was writing and editing my first book, I felt like a kid. I didn't know what I was doing. I sat at my computer, frustrated and stumbling and wishing the words would come easier. It felt embarrassing. But I felt young. Nervous and awake. I liked that part.

I have learned that work feels like work before it becomes flow and art.

I DON'T SURF well. But I have surfed and hung out with lots of surfers. And one thing I know about surfers is that they talk about surfing. A lot.

In some little way, I understand. I've caught a wave a few times and felt the sensation of being lifted, and there is nothing like it. It is the power of the entire ocean, pulled and pushed by the moon and storms and wind, picking you up. It is one of the best metaphors I've ever felt in my body.

In our lives, we have to do a bit of work. If all you do is get in the way of the waves of life, you will be tumbled like laundry. You have to put on that uncomfortable wet suit and paddle through the foam and the muck of a shore break. Get out beyond these messy waves.

Then, once you're there, you still have work to do. You have to turn your board with the swells now behind you. And you trust that your wave will come. It's a bit of guesswork. You see the swell coming, you paddle in spasms, and often you will miss. The wave rolls under you and leaves you. Your arms are tired, but you turn your board and paddle back out again, back to position.

But I promise you, even as someone who has succeeded in this effort only a few times: When you catch it, or it catches you, it feels as though God's hand has come under you to support you. It is a feeling that's gotten millions of people addicted to surfing. It's no hobby or sport. It's love.

But I feel this metaphor everywhere. The callings of our lives have their own uncomfortable wet suits, paddling, cold water, getting through the muck. Then waiting and believing. Then, when you're prepared and in position, the whole damn ocean lifts you and it's no longer you. The entire world is moving, taking you somewhere. You're carried.

I GOT AN email last year that I'll never forget. A woman wrote to say that her mother had just passed away. A few hours before her death, the woman had read her mother some of my words. Something I had written about life and death and returning to the universe we belong to. She said it helped. Then she asked if she could read it at the memorial service.

What do you say to that? How does someone receive an honor like this?

I will always remember where I was standing when I read that email. Because it reminded me of the power of words. The letters and sounds we string together to make sense of living. How they are given away, to be taken and used and laid on top of other lives.

Our words, spoken or written, bend reality. When you joke and say "I'm a lazy person," you utter a prophecy. What starts as playful words becomes a curse. It works the other way, too. When you see a kindness done—even just once—you can say, "Wow, how kind you are!" and bend the person's life in the direction of kindness. He may have been a sour rat for a decade, all because he'd been called horrible things.

To bless or to curse. When you write in your journal, when you talk to your friends and tell stories—when you obsess over your broken heart, the co-worker you can't stand, or your shitty job—you bend the universe. You influence how you see yourself, your community, your future.

Words are sorcery. And we throw them around like dust in the air.

I see words as exfoliation, as healing, as naming the foggy demons that pull my strings. I see them as power. As chances to lift my friends into warm understanding as I try to lift myself. I try to treat them with respect.

"You think you're better than us? You think you're big stuff now?" I wonder how many talents were smothered by this hometown disease. A community is made by its commonalities, by the sharing of space and circumstances. Change that too much, and you betray the community.

I think of smart kids in poor neighborhoods, of artsy kids who threaten their sense of belonging by pursuing their interests. Who get mocked or dismissed as delusional. They get their knees buckled from behind, and end up choosing family over themselves. I wonder if it grew contempt in their hearts for the people they chose. If they felt atrophied by this diminishment, and felt it forever, and took it out on those who clipped their wings.

"The key ingredient of genius is focus."

I've never lived in a different time, but I can tell you that it feels like there is too much information now to focus on anything. I'm expected to know what's happening in Moscow and Georgia and to polar bears and in my sister's backyard and with gluten and school zones and gun laws and populism and taxes. I'm given games and a camera and a message board in my pocket. I'm told of a thousand careers and maybe I'm lucky to have one.

If only I could focus.

If you are interested, you pay attention. If you are fidgety or bored or maybe just hungry, your mind will wander off. Especially since we're all addicted to the sensation of novelty. Research made famous by Kent Berridge at the University of Michigan shows that dopamine is released when something new and potentially useful triggers the brain. We often think dopamine is the stuff of pleasure, but Berridge's research shows that dopamine is related to pleasure, but not pleasure itself. It's a chemical message that says, "Give me more!" And it's activated by sex, many drugs, chocolate, and novelty. The buzz of the phone in your pocket, wondering if it's good news or bad, the endless potential of what you *could* learn from the next Instagram story you swipe through, triggers dopamine release in a way similar to methamphetamine and lust. This, as I'm sure you have noticed, is very distracting.

On most days, and in most hours in the day, I have lost the ability to focus. I will sit down to write, and my phone will not only alert me with texts, but also push notifications from *The New York Times, Los Angeles Times,* Venmo, Gmail, Instagram, Twitter, WhatsApp, NPR, and Chase Bank. If it isn't breaking news, like the number of jobs added to the U.S. economy in September, it's a statement for my checking account or an update in the PayPal user agreement. It's a friend laughing over my Instagram story and then texting me about lunch plans. I need to renew my passport and respond to my cousin about wedding travel. This form of busyness is like cleaning your room instead of writing that college paper. You feel accomplished, but it's not the work you're supposed to be doing.

I try to do one task, to be good and focus on it, but then I take little breaks to check my phone or even switch the song in my headphones. Nothing huge. I think it's harmless. It is not. Research by Sophie Leroy at the University of Washington warns us that this results in what she calls "attention residue." The brain has trouble leaving behind what it was just looking at. When you shift your attention, even if it's just a quick glance at your phone, it clogs the flow of deep thought, and your productivity falls when you return to the main task. The effect can last for ten or more minutes, even if the break was momentary. How many incredible creations are we losing to the insatiable sugar high of shallow communication and information?

I have turned off almost all push notifications on my phone. I write and think clearest in the mornings, so I decided to turn off my phone after my first coffee and leave it out of my writing spaces until one P.M. every day. I've been doing this for a few months now. Some days I don't do it. I am weak in the face of the addiction and find some reason to bring my phone in, for music, or for entertainment on a bathroom break. But when I am true to my commitment to focus, it works. I get twice or three times the writing done.

I think there is a coming reckoning with all this distraction. Middle school classes about phone etiquette and social media behavior will be ubiquitous. There will be a luddite revolution.

. . .

I SAW A couple of articles bemoaning the loss of productivity caused by the total eclipse that crossed over the United States in 2017. Something like $700 million lost because of "distracted employees." The idea made me laugh. That we could even have the conversation. Something as miraculous and strange as the sky going black at 1:30 P.M. for two minutes happens, and we talk about money. I mean, it is interesting to know how much a few minutes of 300 million people's time is worth, I guess. But the fact that, while our country is suffering a complete political bifurcation, the sky would go black and invite every single human being in its path to stop for a few minutes and gaze upward together—it feels like a bit of a miracle, a cosmic gift. And it sliced right across the whole damn country as if on purpose.

As I stood there looking up in a field outside of Nashville, I thought about how lovely unity is. I also thought about how simple the equation is: We need a universal, unusual experience. A clear and present danger, or a clear and present awe. Unity is averse to complexity. Science and race and cultural narratives are muddled, and our animal brains struggle to agree. But a big black orb in the sky, the strangeness of the sun being shut off for two minutes—wow, we can all grasp that.

I thought about the people I was with on that day, their component parts of joy, curiosity, kindness, gratitude, and mischief. How I get to live life with them and cry with them. Usually at beauty.

I don't know if unity like that will be common for us in the future. We get our news from a million different sources. Our interests are now so siloed and specified by algorithms, we no longer listen to the same superstar musicians or read the same books. It's like the world came together for a while in the twentieth century, then started returning to the million tribes we used to be. How this relates to us, and how we will move through life as individuals, I am not sure. It may be that our goals will become smaller. To succeed within our tribes. To impress like-minded consumers. And once in a while, to stop and look at an eclipse, or the last melting glacier, and wonder who all these strangers are that are standing next to us.

DISAPPOINTMENT OFTEN FOLLOWS after achievement. Why do so many artists sink into depression after they win that Grammy or Oscar? Why do entrepreneurs sabotage their marriages and families after they build and sell their companies and win-win-win all that money? Why do successful people drink themselves to death, work themselves to death, shovel the waves of the ocean as if they're making any progress?

I think some people become successful for the very reasons that will ruin them. They were convinced of unworthiness at a young age, were picked on or disregarded, and some foundational building block of "Fuck you! I'll show you! Watch me win!" made it into the basement of who they are.

But man, what a tragedy. The direction of their life, the obsession with money or fame or excess, was set by some sour moment in middle school, by a father's misguided expectations, by a culture's idolatry of wealth as a substitute for purpose in life. They found themselves hungry for meaning in their young bellies, and someone told them that the ultimate meal—junk food and candy—was waiting for them at the top of this long ladder.

Isn't it strange, though, that we are absolutely soaked with warnings of this? Endless books and interviews of successful people shouting "Listen! I did all the things I was supposed to do, and ended up depressed and empty. Get off the assembly line! Jump ship!" But in our youth, we can't hear it. It's as if spiritual knowledge must be earned from watching our shallow pursuits crash and burn.

There seems to be some cosmic formula. Some endless whisper, so repetitious that it's invisible to us until we purchase it with failure. "You must be dumb first," it says. "You must aim for the wrong things. There is no avoiding it. You must pluck the rose and watch it die. Only then will you understand that stealing the rose was never the goal. The goal was to turn you into a gardener."

The universe teaches us in a way that is almost funny. It says, "You will start your life believing that the external world can make you happy. I can't tell you otherwise. You were wired that way. I will tell you early on that it isn't true, but you won't hear me. You will go and chase all that money. And you just might get it. And then, once you've become your own god, exerted your expertise on the world; when your beauty got you sex and power, when your brain got you respect, when your hard work got you a castle; when you've done what you said you would do, you will have some dark realizations. You'll feel the emptiness of space for the first time. How much of it is nothingness. And then, finally, you will listen for me. And if you haven't boarded up your ears, you will hear."

. . .

HAVE YOU EVER had someone, in the heat of being flustered or mad or drunk, belittle you by saying something like "I make more money than you," or "At least I found someone, and won't die alone"? All of a sudden, you realize that they have been thinking like that all along, finding secret labels and rankings to comfort themselves in their envy. I think we're all guilty of this on some level. I know I am. When I felt ugly as a teenager, I consoled myself by thinking, "It's okay, at least I have a good personality. Beauty is fleeting and shallow." Mind you, I was miserable and jealous and wanted to have what the pretty people had. I belittled them in my head to keep from hating myself.

We make these petty rankings, these sad chess moves, because our egos are tortured by the fear of inadequacy. Always trying to be above—or at least not below.

As I've grown up and found myself, I've quit doing this. My mind is much quieter now. I see beauty, and I'm glad that beautiful people exist. I see talent, and I'm glad to see the things that it makes. I don't take someone else's excellence as a challenge to my own. I'm just going to do what I love, make it as good as I can, and love all the lovable things around me. I may never make a masterpiece, and that's okay. There's room for nice things, simple and good things. For grandma's cookies. They never won any awards, but they made that kitchen smell wonderful.

There is so much room. I don't see why we think the landscape of identity is an arms race.

. . .

MY FRIEND MARIANA recently described money to me as a form of energy. It is not meant to be stored up, but to flow and to make things work and movement happen. The root of the word "currency" is *current*. A sustained electric charge that is hot and fast and will kill you if you try to hold on to it. I think fame works in the same way.

Have you seen the documentary *Amy*? About Amy Winehouse? It's devastating. The incredible trove of home videos of Winehouse before fame, interacting with her friends in intimate and tender ways. You really like her. All I remember was when "Rehab" came out, and then came the clips of her drinking herself into a stupor. Horrible concerts, ghastly weight loss. I remember making jokes about her. And the documentary shows that she knew, even before it all, that she couldn't handle it. When asked early in her career how she would handle fame, she said, "I don't think I'm gonna be at all famous. I don't think I could handle it. I'd probably go mad. You know what I mean? I would go mad."

When fame and money are focused through too fragile a wire, it can blow the circuit beyond repair. We give these forces to people, and pretty much hope it fries them.

MY FRIEND TOM said something that I think about often. He said: "Your generation has an idolatry of magnitude. You think if you don't change the world, or reject the world, or make the most money, or give away the most money, or reach the most fame, or throw everything out, or master everything, you have failed. It is an obsession with extremes."

. . .

I WAS ON a run through my neighborhood, listening to Krista Tippett interview Elizabeth Gilbert for her podcast, *On Being.* Yes, I listen to quiet, mumbling podcasts while I run. I enjoy getting lost in words and realizing I'm in a random neighborhood by the end of the episode. The beat of music is too easy to ignore.

Elizabeth Gilbert was discussing life after *Eat, Pray, Love,* a book that was so big, she knows with certainty that she'll never write a book that outsells it. She's now several books past that, working on the speaking circuit, and hosting a podcast of her own.

I was thinking about how much I would love to be a successful writer like her. To sell a million books. To go on massive book tours. To have this or that. But the next thought landed like a falling tree in my path. It felt like a conversation with God.

"What is the difference between that future and now?" the voice said.

"I don't know," I thought. "Money? Ownership of stuff? Notoriety? I guess. It's weird to think that out loud."

"You live in a great house right now. You can afford craft cocktails and gas for your car. You travel constantly. Do you think owning property will improve your life?"

"Hmm . . . I mean, it's what people do. It's what I'm supposed to want, and I do want it. I think."

"Listen, a season of financial security may or may not come, and that's fine. But you know your true dream is to write and connect those words to your heart and the hearts of others. That's why you're here. You know that. And you do that already. Nothing will satisfy you more than that. You already have the thing you're seeking."

When I was done being scolded by this lovely thought, I looked up and realized I was lost in Echo Park. And was reminded that I live in the best neighborhood in Los Angeles.

I LOVE HOW human beings are always specializing. We have inarticulate urges that cause us to split ways. One person wants to write. One person loves organizing. One is a maximizer. One uses her hands. One is physically strong and proud of his stamina. One is a small-moment cherisher. One person loves to film. We often have these urges from the earliest years. If you are a mother or a father, you know. Your kid loved things for seemingly no reason. Obsessed over them. They were the seeds of her future skills.

WHY DON'T THEY teach straightforward life skills in school? Maybe some schools do this, but I don't remember learning much about the nuts and bolts of living when I was a kid. How to pay taxes and what they are and why. How to fix things. How motors work. How funerals work. How much it costs to have a child. How to bury your parents. How to buy your first house. How to manage college debt. How to love imperfect family members. How to see the love and support of your parents as an unwarranted miracle instead of an annoyance or expectation. How to recover from heartbreak. How to find identity in what you do and who you are, rather than what has happened to you. How to find friends who make you more yourself, rather than less. How tiny choices can be seeds that grow into massive unalterable problems. How you can be held accountable for the rest of your life for a brief moment of lust, bravado, or ignorance. How the idea of God's will can be a placeholder for so many people's selfish choices or fears. How happy you can feel to belong, even if it's to the wrong group. How attraction evolves as you grow up. How all things are teaching you all things. How no lie can last.

IMAGINE BEING A meter maid, or a "parking enforcement officer." The consequence of your job is to upset people. If you interact with a "customer," it is a person pleading for leniency, begging in the name of humanity, but you're obligated to do your job, which is to enforce parking rules. If meter maids didn't exist, cars would be left everywhere on any corner forever, and the city would be a big mess.

I've almost never gotten a ticket I didn't deserve. I just misread the sign or lost track of time or whatever. It was never the officer's fault. I can't imagine the emotional toll it must take on someone to be yelled at, begged, raged at every day. This person has a job that feeds their family and pays their rent, and the price is public hatred.

Everyone you see is a human being, trying to make their way.

But this insight takes us only so far. Everyone is a human being, yes. But some human beings are doing shitty things. The excuse of "feeding your family" is used to justify every horrible type of thing. The coal miner destroying forests and mountains is feeding his family. The oil fracker in the virginal Arctic of Alaska. The fisherman driving sharks to extinction. I've got to feed my family. And if the ecosystem collapses? If the world warms up to the point where your family suffers and dies from global collapse and famine?

We didn't evolve to be such a massive pulsing influence on this planet. Our individual instinct to prioritize our immediate family compounds a few billion times into human society at large, and the consequences can devastate. Everyone is a human, doing what they can to survive. Sometimes what we do is annoying. That poor meter maid. But sometimes what we do is destructive, and we have to do better. We can empathize and understand, but if we cannot find a way to feed our families today that doesn't destroy our ability to feed them in a hundred years, there will be a lot fewer people to empathize with.

WATER, OVER TIME, destroyed the smooth land of northern Arizona and made it beautiful. It made the Grand Canyon. I'm sure the land was upset as it happened. Now it boasts.

The flow of your experiences, both planned and unplanned, will carve away the life you thought you'd lead. But it's busy, slowly, slowly, working.

A problem rightly stated is half solved.
—SIDNEY ARMOR REEVE

I keep applying this to everything I think about, from my career to immigration to race to faith to family to sexuality. Information comes to us these days like a fire hose to the face. Especially when we're trying to keep up with the Twitter news cycle. But that quote about asking the right questions captures the utility of curiosity. I want to understand. I want to read and research and ask until I get ahold of something. Not expertise, but the general shape of it. A framework. Then I can start the work of finding an answer. Of mapping it onto my experience. Often, that work is done in the subconscious.

When I was wrestling with Christian scripture and faith and my sexuality, I read and read and read. But then I lived. It wasn't like a light switch went on one day, or a veil got pulled from my eyes. It was a molecular change, atom by atom. The discomfort in my spirit, the feeling that I was living in the limbo of some untruths, piqued my brain's attention—even when I wasn't trying to focus on it consciously. You know when a friend buys a new car, a model you've never seen, and then the next day you see six of them? That's because your brain wasn't looking for the pattern before. When you teach your brain what to look for, acknowledge what's bugging your spirit, and give it language, the pattern-recognition software comes online.

As I read and sought out my questions, my brain awakened. My gut learned first. My head followed much later.

If you are overwhelmed, if you are in the valley between doing and knowing and feeling, try to stay curious. Stop looking for the answers. You need to keep living and let the subconscious collect all of its clues. Do not freeze and wait until you are given a sign.

EVERY GOOD THING you dream of comes with a bad thing in tow. It is the demand of the universe: balance.

I try to consider all my hopes and dreams with that truth

in mind. It keeps me from worshipping them. From creating idols. When I dream of finding a partner, I remember that marriage is hard. That the cost of warm companionship and a proud life together is the sacrifice of my whims, the lordship of my unfettered desires. When I dream of having kids, I remember that raising children is arduous. When I dream of writing books that have an audience, I remember that some people will hate my words, and those comments will make it feel like everyone hates them.

My friend Carolyn said that she wants to ask people who've achieved their dreams, "Tell me about the shadow." The shame they feel for hating parts of the things they thought would save them. They grew up poor and finally hit it rich. And still, life is hard. They tried so hard to have a baby. They prayed and begged and it finally happened. And the kid is a little asshole. They dreamed of owning a restaurant. They saved and remortgaged the house. And today, they dread going to the restaurant they built. Sometimes they want to burn it down.

Think of the relief it'll bring people to discuss it. The freedom of honest exhale.

I don't want my dreams to become perfect, untouchable gods. I want to keep them here on earth to free myself from the fantasy of perfection. I want to finally meet my life, with its natural earthly blemishes, and recognize it for the beautiful balanced thing it's always been.

As a travel writer, you can see the world and make money at the same time. You live an untethered dream. You are the envy of weekend warriors and mothers bound to needy children. But everything has a shadow; everything has a cost. Traveling all the time can cost you a community. You'll miss the intimacy that comes from unscheduled drop-ins from neighbors and friends. You'll miss watching your friends raise their kids. You'll miss being a regular at a coffee shop. You'll miss the feeling of knowing a city or neighborhood is *yours*. A life of freedom too easily becomes an endless buffet of shallow experiences. You may gain the world and its wonders, but you might be trading the riches of belonging.

I don't know much to be absolutely true, but I do believe in balance. Stay rooted too long, and you could lose your wonder. Stay gone too long, and you could lose your depth.

Death

Meme (pronounced "Me-Me") was the type of grandmother any kid would wish for. On our visits to her house, she would have me stand on a stool next to her so we could make doughnuts together. She would cuss under her breath to punctuate a story, and wink at me. When my little brother and I got too rowdy, running around her house and yelling, she would brandish a knife and threaten to cut off our legs. She was funny, clever, and kind to us. Both strong as a storm and as gentle as sunrise. She had the soft wrinkled skin a grandmother is supposed to have. And though her hands were warped by arthritis, her crooked pinkies were my favorite. They were crooked not from the arthritis but from genetics. I inherited those crooked pinkies and always felt they added something to my love for her.

My mom, Meme's daughter, had a different experience with her. She says Meme was a very tough mother. Critical and cold. Meme never once told my mother that she loved her. I was shocked when Mom first told me this. To my siblings and me, Meme was a bottomless well of love.

When I was a kid, Mom regularly drove us the five hours from Nashville to Poplar Bluff, Missouri, to spend a weekend or a week with Meme and Papa. I'm sure Meme's help watching us kids made the long drive worth it for my mother. She raised us mostly on her own, and didn't have that kind of help in Tennessee. I have memories from those visits of my mother and Meme sitting in the kitchen, talking about adult things. This would happen every time we went. While playing or watching TV or hiding from my brother, I would walk past the two of them as they discussed the many confusing variables of adulthood. Meme had a sharp, hard voice, and spoke the way a woman would if she no longer cared to impress anyone. She always sounded self-assured. Above the bullshit of the world. My mom's gentle, feminine voice on one side of the conversation, describing the unfairness of it all, and Meme, street-smart and raspy, telling her to fight and kill.

I started going bald at seventeen, likely due to the medicine I was taking for acne. It dried up my skin to help with breakouts, but its side effects were brutal. Suicidal thoughts. And my hair fell out in chunks. The shower drain got so clogged, it looked like I'd buzzed my entire head in there. I'm sure I would've gone bald no matter what; my dad is bald as hell. But at seventeen? That's intense. What's worse, my hair had always been thick before it started to fall out. Every time I got it cut, the barber would compliment me. Amazed at how much there was.

To save money, Meme started cutting my hair whenever I went to her house. I sat in a wooden chair in her kitchen, maybe eighteen years old, as Meme snipped at the wispy strands of hair left behind from the Accutane genocide. I was self-conscious about her looking at my scalp, but she treated me like the barbers had always done. "You know, you have the most beautiful head," she said. "The shape of it. God didn't want all that hair blocking out the shape of your head. People need to see this head." She said it as if it were the most obvious thing in the world.

Ten years ago, Meme had a stroke. Suddenly, the grandmother I knew was gone. She could no longer speak or walk or wash herself. She cooed in falsetto all day. There was no melody in those vocalizations. Just notes, like a broken songbird.

She was a baby again.

We spent the Christmas of 2010 visiting Meme in the nursing home, with my mom bathing her and petting her and holding her hand. My sister did, too. The nursing home felt like a hospital. White walls. Beige doors. Fluorescent lights. Metal handrails running along the walls. And moaning and crying and shouting coming from behind doors. We sat in Meme's sterile room and talked to her. She couldn't make eye contact. It felt like there was no one home to look back at you.

As caretakers, my mom and sister came alive. My mother put photos and flowers all over the room. She brought Meme's favorite things, knickknacks and treasures from her house, and lined them on the windowsill. We tried teaching her to walk again. We wrapped her arms around our necks and then lifted her up and held her on her feet as she shuffled across the floor. I held up her weight almost completely, but I could feel her weak legs pumping as she tried to stand. I knew her brain was broken and probably gone, but I told her how much I loved her right in her ear. "You're doing such a great job, Meme." She would make a high-pitched coo and rest her warm, soft skin on my cheek.

A couple days into the visit, something strange happened. As we scooted across the floor, between the endless howls of Meme's neighbors, she got quiet for a second, and a charge went through her body, as if her muscles were working in concert again. Then she whispered, "Thank you," in my ear. Not in her baby voice, but in her real voice. I pulled back so I could look into her face, but it was too late. She became soup again, staring into space and hitting high notes.

"Mom!" I said. "Meme just said, 'Thank you!' In my ear!"

"I knew it," my mom said. She walked up to Meme and petted her. "She's in there, trying to talk to us. She's in there. 'Mother, we love you, we're here, we won't leave you. We'll get you walkin' again. We're right here.' "

Nobody dreams of spending Christmas in a nursing home. But for four days, our whole family had one mission: to love and help Meme. Looking back now, it was the best Christmas of my life.

MEME DIED SEVEN months later.

By then, she and Papa had been married for sixty-seven years. They'd slept in the same bed for nearly seven decades. Not a king-size bed. Not a queen. A double bed. When Meme died, we didn't know what Papa would do. He was ninety years old and alone. Meme had been all energy. She would complain about Papa loud enough for him to hear from the other room, as if she was doing a stand-up routine for him, about him. Papa moved quietly, read *Popular Science* magazine in his La-Z-Boy, and watched Westerns. By the time I was old enough to pay attention, I never saw Meme and Papa engage each other. I mean really look at each other. They made little jokes that got the other one to chuckle. Fart jokes or halfhearted threats of divorce. They'd talk about gas prices and my aunt Vicky and their two little yipping dogs. Their relationship wasn't kisses and holding hands—maybe that's how they were for the first forty years, but by now it was settled coexistence. Two humans who became one comfortable thing, sitting beside each other in recliners watching Barbara Walters. They were as joined as the land and sky. And now Meme was gone.

My mom hired a caretaker to move in and help Papa around the house, but I wondered how long he would survive without his wife. In the end, he made it two years. A brain tumor grew in the darkness of his skull, unknown to anyone, until one day I got a call from my mother saying Papa was at the hospital for emergency surgery. They soon learned it was inoperable. The next day, he was in a coma. Mom said the doctors would try to keep him on life support long enough for the family to say goodbye. But it was likely he would die any day. Any minute.

When we talked, I was in Washington, D.C., about to host a youth conference for the nonprofit where I worked. Four thousand people were going to attend. I was one of the emcees. I debated with myself, and floated the idea of leaving. My co-workers were sympathetic. They told me I could leave if I wanted to, but I knew they didn't want me to. And in some buried way, I didn't want to leave, either. I have always been averse to extreme awkward emotions, to death and sadness. I guess we all are. I do not rush in to help. I hide in busyness. To be brutally honest, I think I hoped Papa would die and I would miss the drama of it all and then get there for the funeral. I didn't think this with clear thoughts. I just told myself, "I can't miss the conference. I'm the emcee. These kids are expecting me."

I called Mom and told her I couldn't skip the conference.

"I am one of the faces of the whole thing," I said. She understood. "Papa knows you love him. The funeral will be next week, so just come straight here when you're done."

The conference was in three days. I got an update on Papa every day. He was hanging on. He saw my brother, my sister, his two daughters, his nieces and nephews. When I say he "saw" them, it was more that they came by and held his hand and said goodbye. In that hospital bed, he was silent and still. The doctors said there was nothing going on in his head. That the tumor had killed his brain. They moved him out of the hospital and into hospice care in his home.

The conference came and went. On Sunday afternoon, I went to the airport to fly to St. Louis, rent a car, and drive the rest of the two hours from there. I called my mom on the way to Poplar Bluff. "The doctors are amazed that he's hung on this long," she said. "I think he's waiting on you, Jed. You're the only one that hasn't said goodbye."

As I drove through the dark Missouri countryside, I wondered how Papa would look when I saw him. Would he be swollen or green? Or just asleep? I got there around midnight. Mom came and met me on the front porch. She looked ecstatic.

"About thirty minutes ago, he started shaking and convulsing," she said. "He hasn't moved an inch in days. His spirit knew you were coming." I walked into the house and saw my grandfather. A hospital bed had been moved into the living room, in the exact place where his La-Z-Boy had been for decades. Papa was in his spot. Only his hand was wiggling. My mom was beaming, "He is so happy you're here. He waited for you, Jed."

The hospice nurse was standing beside him. "You can

hold his hand, talk to him, it's fine. This is special. He hasn't moved in days," she said.

I walked toward him, or floated, really. It felt surreal. I took Papa's hand and he stopped shaking.

By that point, I knew his brain was mush. I believed the doctors who read the charts and saw that there was nothing inside. But as I held his warm, strong hands—hands that had always seemed made of wood—I remembered Meme's thank-you and wondered if something was still in there. I mean, he was shaking for me, right?

"I love you, Papa," I said. "You set such a good example of what a man should be. Noble. Kind. A good husband. Wise. Hardworking. I'm so honored to be your grandson. I love you."

That's all I had. He had been such a quiet man, I hardly knew him in the way I know most people. But I did love him. He was less a string of words than a presence. A sturdiness. An eternal, calm present. I looked to my mom, gave a flat-lipped smile, and nodded. She took his other hand and leaned over him.

"Okay, Daddy, everyone's come and said their goodbyes. You can go now. You can go be with Meme. We love you so very much."

He lay there, perfectly still with the oxygen tube in his nose. His eyes closed. I wondered if he heard anything. I assumed he did not. But I believe in symbolism, ritual, and what it meant to us to say goodbye. To feel the blood in his still-warm hands. To get our peace for us.

I went to the guest bedroom and set my bag down. That night, Mom would sleep in the bedroom where Meme and Papa had slept for decades. The hospice nurse would stay with Papa in the living room—sleep on the couch, I assumed. I brushed my teeth and crawled under the covers, but as I leaned to turn off the lamp and sleep, the door opened. It was Mom.

"Jed. He really did wait for you. He's gone. The nurse just told me."

I leapt up and followed her to the living room. Papa was dead. "He was waiting for you," Mom repeated. "He's with Meme now."

We went into the kitchen with the hospice nurse. My mom made tea.

"Does this happen a lot?" I asked the nurse.

"It does. Often the person who is unconscious, or seems to be, will wait for someone specific. I've even seen them wait for someone to leave the room, someone they don't like."

"I thought the doctors said he was brain-dead," I said.

"It's very hard to know what's going on in there," the nurse said.

But my mom, after all she'd seen that week, wasn't in doubt. "His soul was still in there," she said.

Do you know the names of your great-grandparents? What about your great-greats? What were their names? What did they do for work? I bet many of you don't. That's only four generations away, a hundred years ago. You are their legacy. Their children's children's children's children, and you don't even know them. What does it mean to disappear? Someday, you will be forgotten, too.

There is an app called WeCroak that reminds you five

times a day that you will die. It sends you a random push notification with a quote like, "Death is only the end if you assume the story is about you." Or, "People are born soft and weak. They die hard and stiff." The intent is to promote contemplation and prioritization of time. If you are reminded that you will die, perhaps you won't stress so much when you can't finding a parking spot, or when Jessica doesn't return your text. My friend Joey uses the app and says he likes it. I do not use it. I am afraid it would put too much dread on me, inject too much intensity into moments that deserve to be silly. Sometimes I want to be annoyed at simple things.

But I do think it's important to do just what that app does. To remind yourself that you will die, and because of that absolute fact, some things matter more than others.

I say "absolute fact," but I know that scientists and billionaires in Silicon Valley are, as I type, trying to solve the problem of aging. It is believed that we age because of something called the Hayflick limit. Human cells stop dividing properly (that is, copying themselves exactly) after around fifty divisions. After that magical number, small bits of DNA are lost when your body replaces its cells. This is aging.

Some cells do not do this. The Hayflick limit is not universal. It is programmed in there for some reason, and scientists want to turn it off. Or maybe even reverse its effects. At some point, aging might become something that happens only to the poor. What could result is a very strange dystopia. Without the certainty of aging and death, death would come only by mistake or boredom. The rich would take far fewer risks. You wouldn't have to die of old age, but you could still die in a plane crash or burn to ash in a house fire. Or fall off a cliff. And then we might observe the existential dread that comes from living nine hundred years and becoming bored, literally, to death.

Even then, I think that famous statement from Steve Jobs would apply: "Remembering that you are going to die is the best way I know to avoid the trap of thinking you have something to lose. You are already naked. There is no reason not to follow your heart."

Whether death is inevitable or elective or feared, it will retain its true power: Death is what gives life meaning. The act of not being alive makes being alive special. There is no light without darkness. There is no waking without sleep.

Maybe that weird app is on to something.

I FOLLOW A very disturbing account on Instagram. It's called Nature Is Metal. It is simply photos and videos of animals brutalizing each other. A snake swallowing another snake. A praying mantis catching a hummingbird and eating it alive. A baby gazelle stooping down to drink from brown water, and the water becomes the mouth of a fourteen-foot crocodile. The captions highlight the meaninglessness of death in the animal kingdom. The absolute vacuum of dignity. "Komodo dragon slamming a monkey down the yapper," or, "Yoink. Python ambushes a juvenile deer at the local watering hole."

Why do I follow it? Because I have a young boy's morbid fascination with death and gore, and because there is something less repugnant about violence between animals. The morality is taken out. They were designed to do this. The spider evolved fangs to tear into a bug's beautiful shell and kill it. That's nature doing its thing. And it isn't always for

food. In one video, I watched a hippopotamus drown a gazelle for no reason.

The crocodiles are my favorite to watch. They elicit the
same horror in me as great white sharks—killing machines
so far removed from us that we see no mind working in their
eyes. No language or emotion. Just a blackness that will kill
you. A crocodile comes from the water, just like a shark, but
his water is brown. You can't see one inch through it. He
moves invisibly and takes brutal advantage of an animal's
most basic need: drinking water.

One post shows a zebra surrounded by crocodiles after a
fight. They are all in the water, the zebra's nearly dead body
laid across the backs of a few crocs. The zebra is moving only
slightly, clearly tired from the struggle. As you look, you see
that the zebra's nose and mouth have been ripped off. The
top half of its head is normal zebra, black-and-white stripes,
down to its eyes. But just below the eyes, a few inches down,
the bottom half is gone. All that is left is pink flesh and white
skull. A bit of flesh from its cheek is pulled taught in a croc's
mouth, and the croc is trying to rip it away.

In that video, the crocodiles do not seem hurried or even
very interested. They move slowly while the zebra rests on
them and weakly pulses, making small objections to being
eaten. One crocodile lumbers up and tries to bite the zebra's
large rump, but can't get his mouth around.

The caption reads, "Welcome to hell. Nature doesn't give
a flying fuck about your feelings."

As a kid in church, I was taught that the garden of Eden
was a real place. It had no death. Lions lay with lambs. Ev-

erything lived in peace, and lived forever. It was the sin of Eve, and then Adam, that brought death to all.

This story was always hard for me. If the lion lays down with the lamb instead of killing it, what will his cubs eat? Grass? With those huge sharp teeth? Some Christian writers and teachers, including C. S. Lewis, have believed the story was metaphor. That evolution was real and that the story of Adam and Eve was a hypersimplified story given to us by God to convey His creative glory. That felt right to me. But others, like my pastor in college, believed that the story was not a metaphor. It was exactly true.

That pastor was perhaps the only true genius I've ever met. He had a photographic memory, and his cohesive comprehension of the Bible was a supernova to behold. He could sew dozens of passages together into a sermon, having us flip from Genesis to Jeremiah to Revelation without ever looking at his notes. Any question you asked, he could answer with a waterfall of Bible verses. They came to him from the top of his head like flits of lightning. People asked about heaven and hell. About divorce. About specific verses that confused them.

One morning, after the church's sunrise Bible study, I asked, "If there was no death before the fall, then why do so many animals have specific features designed for death? Like a snake's fangs? Or a scorpion's tail? Or a spider's web? What did these animals look like in Eden without these important parts of them?"

The genius pastor didn't hesitate. "All of creation was distorted at the moment of the fall," he said. "Death came not just for Adam and Eve, but for all the world. So in that moment, the brutality of killing came to the animal kingdom."

"So they, like, morphed?"

"We don't know exactly. It could have happened in an instant. God could change all of creation in the blink of an eye, and we wouldn't know. But maybe a morphing, yes."

Wow. A cuddly spider morphing into a murder machine before our eyes. This answer ignited a curiosity in me. *Hmmm, I didn't think of it like that.* And yet I couldn't buy it. It's just too . . . forced. Reverse engineered to make the Bible story work. I've always found the explanation, "With God all things are possible," to be annoying. It shuts down thinking. Which is perhaps the point.

Besides, the most interesting parts of these animals are the parts that kill. The brilliant stripes of the tiger are there so it can hide when it hunts. Were they an afterthought of the fall? The neon colors of the poison dart frog are a warning. If you eat it, you will die. The streamline of a shark. The speed of the falcon. The silent glide of an owl's wing. The deadly talons of the eagle. Did eagles have duck feet in Eden?

What are we to make of all this killing? What makes a man evil and a hippopotamus innocent? Is it the soul? Free will? Consciousness?

The absence of morality in nature is strange. Big cats bite the necks of their victims, suffocating them before they eat them. This feels humane in a way, but biologists believe it's simply an adaptation to protect the cats. A flailing animal could kick you in the face. A dead one is easier to shred. My family's cat used to leave us presents at the back door. I came home from school one day to find a living chipmunk with his belly slit open and his intestines dragging behind him as he slowly tried to crawl off the porch. My cat sat a few feet away, watching. Blank-faced. Proud.

Humans, at least in theory, are held to a higher standard. If we torture a dog, that is wrong. But if an orca flips a seal pup into the sky, we see it as the whale's hunting instinct blending with its instinct to play. When I look closer at *us,* though, at human behavior, it feels like we aren't so different from that orca. If I stab you, I am a bad man. But if I have a blood clot in my brain that drives me mad, and "I" am incapacitated by the seizure of my mind, did I do the stabbing, or was it the blood clot's fault? If I am having a proper muscle spasm and stab you with the kitchen knife in my hand, you probably won't hold that against me. Everything, when inspected closely enough, seems inevitable. Somehow cleansed of moral failure.

I've noticed that most of the movies I grew up with had starkly contrasted villains and heroes. The bad guys were cartoonishly evil. Absent of any complexity. The shark in *Jaws.* Saruman. Voldemort. Ursula. Darth Vader. Then the antihero emerged. The *Star Wars* prequels tried to explain the rise of Vader, and Maleficent, the evil witch from *Sleeping Beauty,* was humanized. Walter White started as a bumbling science teacher, and we watched as his ego turned him into a monster. The Joker became a sad child of neglect and mental illness.

These stories attempt to show that every villain has a backstory, something that *made* them the way they are. In other words, they blur the source of evil, which we often assume is the will of a human soul. They give our bad deeds a spot in the chain of events of reality, an ultimate cause of some twist in the past. A bad mother. An early rejection. They engender a sense of empathy for the villain. The feeling that they'd been wronged. Made into monsters by someone or society.

What makes these stories more tragic is that the injury doesn't have to be the result of choice. There isn't always a senior villain who made the junior villain. There isn't always a malignant cause. How often have I caught feelings for someone who liked me only as a friend? I'll read their kindness as flirting, and then rage at them for not texting me back later that night. But it wasn't their fault. It was a tango of my leaping assumptions, and perhaps their overly compliant kindness—the lingered hand on my shoulder, or even their benign enjoyment of flirtatious energy—that sent me whirling. Where is the evil there? Where is the will?

These little moments feel like micrometaphors for the causes of bigger problems. When brothers hurt each other's feelings, their pride can keep them from apologizing or even speaking to each other for decades. Now take these a few steps up, to the largeness of misunderstandings between groups, and you get disagreements between companies, between church denominations and ethnic groups. Hurt feelings and pride. Miscommunications. Small cuts going unhealed until they fester into wounds. And small lies metastasizing into myths, stories, and legends. Good guys and bad guys. War, genocide, and racism. Some people are rotten to the core—sociopaths and violent dictators—but I think they are far more rare than we assume. Most of the tragedy in human society stems from these smaller rippling hurts. Small and big distrusts compounding and mixing with human desires. And the tension caused by the fact that different people want different things.

I can't find where evil comes from. If it's from the devil, then why are we held responsible? At the shallowest level, we hold people responsible. Adolf is evil. So is the rapist.

They don't get a backstory. Is George W. Bush evil? Many Iraqis must think so. Millions of Americans would say he is not. Who gets to say? When the hurricane comes and rips a tree from the soil, does the tree call the wind and rain evil?

How would I define evil? "That which is not of God"? "That which is against life"? I don't know. But it feels rooted in death. In the fear of death. In the fear of those who cause death.

We cling to life so tightly, don't we? Take a walk through a beautiful forest, and ask the choking kudzu if it is evil. Ask the spider waiting for a moth. Ask the bluebird with a grasshopper in its pretty little beak. Ask the frenzy of death all around you.

The Soul

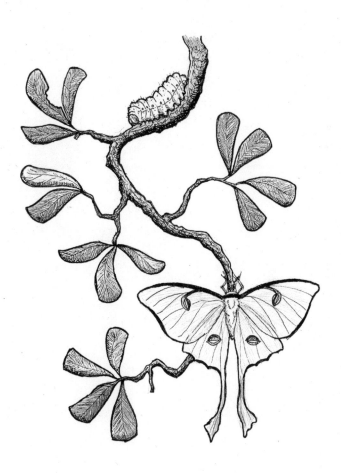

I've never had a spiritual experience. Never heard the voice of God or felt the tangible presence of the divine.

There was a time when I really wanted to speak in tongues, and so I forced myself to do it while I prayed alone, hunched over on my knees in my closet. I have never been good at asking for things, especially from God. Usually I just prayed gratitude. But when someone told me there was a difference between praying in tongues and a "prayer language"—more personal meditation than the foreign language miraculously spoken in church—I was intrigued. So I just started making sounds, "Sha nananananna ra tatatatatataata," and kept going until it felt less willed than inevitable, flowing out of me like a mantra. My mind had been freed from thought and my tongue was released to do whatever it wanted to. For a few moments, I felt separate from the faking. Like I was doing something holy. Talking with God.

Who knows.

I don't know what to make of the spiritual world. I don't know if I believe in it at all. But it is the most profound part of many people's lives. Millions of people, maybe the majority of people on the planet, would say it's the most important thing that matters. And it is the foundation of the family I grew up in. The fact that we are not mere matter, but souls. As that saying goes, "You do not have a soul. You are a soul. You have a body."

This may be true. Matter is neither created nor destroyed. Upon death, we are rearranged into something else. And anyone alive can feel a current of something flowing through them.

I have never died, so I don't know what happens, if anything. But I have believed in my soul, and worried that it would end up in hell. I have believed that God is everywhere and animated our bodies with spirits. I have hoped that Meme's spirit is watching over me. I often still do.

WHEN I WAS nine and my little brother was seven, our family took a road trip from Nashville to Canada. It was a long drive with stops in Missouri, Kansas, South Dakota, North Dakota, Montana, and Alberta. My stepdad, Mike, drove a blue GM Yukon pulling a thirty-foot camper, and my mom sat with him in the front. In the back seat, my sister sat against the window doing something—I can't remember— while my brother and I bickered and teased each other for thousands of miles.

I would covertly tickle him, and he would flail and shout, "Jed won't leave me alone!" By the time my mom spun around, I would be there, book in my hands, sitting perfectly still. "I'm not even touching you," I'd say, the devil in my heart. Sometimes I won. Mom would say, "Luke, calm down and stop!" and Luke, incensed, would look at me in shock. I'd smile at him like Rasputin.

At one point we were driving through some flat stretch of nothing and Luke said, "I really have to poop." We were miles from any gas station or exit. I saw this as the perfect opportunity to tickle him. I guess I didn't project what success would look like. I just knew it would make him miserable. When I tickled him, he screamed, and I heard a fart—a lumpy fart with the resonance of surround sound. Then the car smelled like . . . well, human shit. A rank invasion that left every person in the car screaming. Mike quickly pulled over; Luke's underwear was removed and thrown into a field. I received a proper scolding. And as we drove away, Luke said, "I told you to stop," over and over.

A few days into the trip, we stopped in Rapid City, South Dakota. The campground was big, with RVs and campers and cars parked next to tents. There were sewer hookups and decent showers and a crusty pool. After pulling in late in the afternoon, we walked out the front entrance to eat at a diner down the block. Then we played cards in the RV and went to sleep. Tomorrow, we would get up early to drive to Mount Rushmore.

The camper had two bunk beds in the back, next to the "master bedroom," which was sectioned off by a curtain. The table in the kitchen area collapsed into a bed. Luke and I slept in different bunks, with me on top and him on the bottom. Mom and Mike were in the big bed. And my sister Rebekah was on the table bed by the door.

Both of my siblings were known sleepwalkers. I'd heard stories of my sister crawling around the house on all fours, screaming at the top of her lungs. My brother wasn't that dramatic. He would just walk around the house like a lazy ghost. Silent, emotionless. But I guess they had never sleepwalked away from home, and it wasn't a common enough occurrence for Mom and Mike to worry about it. It happened maybe two times a year. It never crossed anyone's mind that they could walk out of our RV and get lost in the wilderness.

Apparently, at some point that night, Luke got up, walked over to the door with the soft feet of a cat, fumbled it open in silence, and went outside. To do this in a trailer without waking anyone up would've been impossible. We were all within mere feet of one another. But he did it, moving like a silky ninja in his unconscious state.

We don't know at what point in the night he did this. We knew it happened only because there came a knock at the door around four A.M. It was pitch-black outside. A knock on the camper door at that hour is quite jarring. We woke up, confused.

Mike wrenched himself from the bed, put on a T-shirt to accompany his boxers, and walked to the door. He was a stern man with a deep baritone, the voice a water buffalo would have if it spoke English. "Hello?" he said as he leaned to the door with a bothered brow.

"Um, hello," a kind male voice answered from the other side of the door. "I think I may have something that belongs to you."

The door swung open. "Luke!" Mike said. I couldn't see the other man. I saw only Mike's outline in the doorway.

"I had gone to bed when I heard a child crying," the man said. "When I looked outside, there was this little redheaded boy wandering around. He said his name was Luke and I asked where he was from and he said he was either from Missouri or Tennessee. He wasn't sure. I've been searching a half hour for campers from the South."

"Wow. Well, thank you very much," Mike said, his bull-ish tone softened. "I guess we'll lock the door."

"That's a good idea," the man said through a smile big enough to hear. "Well, I'll let you all get some rest. Luke, it was nice to meet you. You stay inside now, okay?"

"Thank you very much," Mike repeated in an awkwardly formal manner, confused by the whole episode. From my bed, I heard the gravel crunch as the man walked away.

Luke was quiet. He stepped into the trailer and Mike locked the door and led him to his bed. I fell asleep to the muffled mumblings of my mother and Mike coming from the back.

The next morning, Mike and my mom were out the door at dawn. They had gone to the front desk to find the man and thank him, but when Mike described the guy to the person behind the counter, it didn't ring a bell. They searched all morning, went camper by camper. There was no sign of him ever having stayed there. Mom and Mike were flum-moxed. Wondering if they'd imagined the whole thing.

"Jed, did you wake up and see that man who brought Luke back last night?" Mike asked when they returned.

"I didn't see him, but I heard him talk."

Mike turned to my mom. "See, at least we know it really happened."

As we drove toward Canada, my mom said, "What if that man was a real angel? Sent by God to protect Luke. He could've walked into traffic or been kidnapped. I bet he was an angel."

. . .

A FEW MONTHS ago, someone asked, "So, are you still a Christian?"

I said yes. But that word means something different to me than it did ten years ago. What have I shed? What have I changed? For one, I no longer crave certainty. The gate-keeping suspicion, "Are you one of us, or not?" is not on my breath. I do not worship the Bible. I see it as a brilliant, messy road map, humanity's search for God. I do not care what name you give to Jesus. I do not care what language you put to the ever-flowing work of God. I tried all that. I shoved God and Jesus into this tiny members-only club—and boy, the two of them rattled that cage. They broke apart these trembling communities, through bickering and atrophy and betrayal. God kept saying, "Why do you labor to defend me? Don't you see I need no protection? I fear no blasphemy. I fear no deception. What is it that you think you're protecting?"

God mocks the teachers who assume He quit speaking two thousand years ago. The ones who scrape their knees as they crawl, begging to follow rules and laws, begging to be told how to live, and ignoring God's commission to rise, look Him in the eye, and accept the invitation to astonishment.

But as I talk about it more, the language loses its shape. I start speaking in generalities. The metaphors are as close as I can get.

I am a Christian. I keep this language because it gives credit where credit is due: It's where I come from. I was raised in a firm and sturdy belief. But I did not stay there. I do not worship the nest in which I hatched. It was there I was fed, and grew my wings. But I am a bird. "Come and see the sky," I heard, long before I knew that's what I was hearing.

HOW COULD THE truth of God be hidden? Or, to say it differently: Why would the spiritually urgent be kept from us? I don't know how I ever rationalized the confusing commission of Paul: *Evangelize the world, save them from hell. Of course, those who never hear the gospel won't go to hell. Those uncontacted tribes in Brazil. But you should still go there and share the good news!* What? Then why would I go? Why would I give someone the option to love Jesus, just to risk them going to hell? If I never gave them the option, they'd be good. Right?

This strange equation, that salvation lies in special knowledge, in a special story, really ate at me. The full truth of the universe must be present on the back of a stupid bug on the sidewalk, or not exist at all.

I've spent so many years feverishly buying books looking for the right teaching, the truest revelation. Maybe C. S. Lewis knows? Maybe Alan Watts? Maybe Carl Sagan? I thought that if I didn't study hard enough, look hard enough, the truth would turn away from me.

Then, it unraveled. God may have hid secret messages, love notes, deep in the trillionth digit of pi. He may have made the universe endlessly interesting. He may have made our souls as deep as deep can go. But he wouldn't withhold salvation. He wouldn't withhold his love behind an unfair game we were born to lose.

I realized: Put down the books for a minute and behold the ant tickling your leg. It is enough. You belong. Relax.

.   .   .

CHRISTIANS OFTEN ASK one another, "How's your relationship with God?" I used to hear it all the time, from one Bible study to the next. I used to ask it a lot, too.

People don't ask me that anymore—most Christians know I'm not exactly one of them—but I'll answer it as if I were. I've never felt closer to God. I've never felt so real, so true. I don't lie to God anymore. I don't use faith as a social scorecard. I know you want me to say something different, something clearer, something more certain, but I'd rather tell the truth.

When I used to ask people that question, I was asking something different. I see this only now. I was probing them to see if they were the same kind of Christian as me. To size them up. To see if they were saved. In the club. I was asking them to see if I was better or worse. I secretly hoped they were praying less than me, going to church less than me.

In my twenties I started to see the rot in my soul. This performative faith that had so much less to do with God and the truth than comfort and being right. I was never afraid of God. I was afraid of my community. Of loneliness. Of abandonment.

I love God, whatever that means. I love you, whatever that means. I love my odd life, and I feel what it means more and more every day. I hope you don't mind me showing my cards the way I do. I've never enjoyed playing to win.

THERE IS A word in Japanese that has no translation in English: *Yūgen*. It is the feeling of the mysterious bigness of the universe. The sad beauty of the pain of living. The fourteenth-century playwright Zeami Motokiyo compared it to wandering "in a huge forest without thought of return." The term originated in Chinese philosophy, where it meant "dim" or "deep." As it integrated into Japanese aesthetic poetry, it took on the meaning of "that which cannot be said." It alludes not to another world, but to the unsayable pulsing meaning of this one.

This is the core of my religious experience. The unsayable. The abstract weight of meaning that lands on us like beauty.

THE WHOLE WORLD can fall apart. Your parents can die, your husband can stop loving you, and all manner of things can go wrong. What we expect from life goes unfulfilled, and often.

But even in the rubble of the worst chaos, if you manage to hang on, there will be a lull in the hell around you. A clear sky and maybe a sunset. If you are given one minute to catch your breath, you might think, "The sky is beautiful." You may feel bad for thinking this when misery has become your reason, when anger at God has become your calling. But you can't help it. Even fire can be beautiful. And rainbows show up in the middle of war. When this happens, the thought that it all might just mean something creeps back in. Even if it's a delusion. It creeps back in.

GROWING UP, WE'RE taught a series of myths. We reject the myths as we age and decide what we really believe. But sometimes we rediscover the myths later, with the benefit of new wisdom.

The story of Adam and Eve really bugged me. What kind of all-knowing creator would set us up for failure? Is the knowledge of good and evil really that bad? As I grew up, my belief in that story didn't last. It didn't make sense. It was too simple. Too human.

Seeing the world as it is today, with billions of humans trying to navigate more information than our monkey brains can process, I look at the story differently. At one time, we lived in the balance of nature. We did that for a very long time. But knowledge came around, and we conquered the world with it. We didn't eat from the tree of the wisdom of the balance of life. It was the tree of the knowledge of good and evil. The tree taught us that things are "this" or "that"— a false binary that has poisoned the world. Right or wrong. Profitable or worthless. Growth or death. Bits of incomplete information. Rumors and clickbait. Confirmation bias. The wolf of emotion in the clothes of reason.

The garden was protecting us from knowledge. And now we worship knowledge above all.

That which can be destroyed by the truth, should be.

—P. C. HODGELL

How liberating. That is where my allegiance lies. The truth. And in the utility of a course correction. If I feel in my heart something is right, I will move in the direction of the rightness. And if I find that I was wrong all along, I will adjust. If I burn my hands, I will pull away.

. . .

IF YOU COULDN'T speak or write, what would your life say? What would those around you say you believe?

I've spent most of my life surrounded by born-again Christians. They believe that the son of God died to save them from their sins, and that this same messiah walked around the Middle East telling people to denounce material wealth, serve the widows and the poor, pick up their cross and follow him. But the Christians from my upbringing—myself included—weren't much different from everyone else. Maybe we didn't have sex before marriage. Maybe we went to church or Bible study (to see our friends). But none of us were giving our coats away or housing widows and refugees. I mean, maybe we donated to Christian organizations that did work like that. Maybe we gave money to a homeless guy or even made sandwiches once a year to pass out. We certainly didn't heed Jesus's warnings about wealth. We loved wealth. We were American, goddamnit.

Actions are the real signifiers of internal conviction.

Imagine if you couldn't tell people what you stood for. Instead, they would look back at the last year of your life, stripped of words, and report back what they saw. Who would you be? Someone who cares about racial justice? Equality? The environment? What did you do this year with your time?

What if they looked only at where you spent your money? People would think my religion is eating out.

. . .

THE PENNSYLVANIA CONSTITUTION has a clause that requires officeholders to believe in a Supreme Being and an afterlife based on reward and punishment. Eight states still have these clauses. The Supreme Court ruled them unenforceable in 1961, but they are still there, reminders of what once was. Some of these clauses made Protestant belief the requirement, as a way to exclude Catholics and Jews from office. Others were safeguards against "dangerous" atheists. But another reason for these clauses was the concept of an omnipotent "watcher." You might lie and trick all those around you, people believed, but God is watching. You cannot deceive God. This felt especially important with police officers, politicians, and judges.

These tests are rightly gone. I don't want one denomination or religion to dominate others. But I wonder what integrity looks like without belief in a "watcher on high." It makes sense to me that a person in power should fear the judgment of their soul. That corruption and duplicity will not stand. But these tests never really worked in the first place. Judges and officers and priests have been abusing power from the very beginning. Torture and murder during the Inquisition. Molestation and cover-ups in last week's *New York Times*. These things are so common, they are almost a feature of organized religion.

But I do believe that integrity in the smallest things has some kind of cosmic dividend. That the measure of good character is how you treat people who can do nothing for you.

Here's a dumb but relevant story: More than once, I've sneezed in my hands and wiped them on the seat of a taxi. It wasn't until now, as I sit down to think about this, that I ever felt bad for doing it. Something subconscious directed me to wipe my fucking snot on a stranger's car, a car that they personally own, simply because they'll probably never see it and definitely never know it was me. My lizard brain took the opportunity for granted. It said, "No one is watching, therefore there is no consequence."

I don't believe in a God who keeps tallies. But I do believe that God is watching, whatever that means. When I act selfishly to the secret detriment of another, the universe listens and sends rotten ripples into the whatever. I am not innocent of those actions, even if it simply means that they accrue in my heart until I feel like a bad person, a coward, and a phony. This belief has consequences. When you decide that you are beyond repair, you acquiesce to the cycle of pain. You hurt others and throw up your hands and say, "What can you expect? This is what I am."

Who we believe ourselves to be is who we become.

"BE THE PERSON you needed when you were younger."

I saw this quote attributed to Banksy, but I don't know who really said it. It seems too cheesy for Banksy, even if it's true.

As a teenager, I needed someone who loved God and science. Who wasn't so certain about things that felt uncertain to me. Who didn't think people were just straight or gay or conservative or liberal or right or wrong, but somewhere on a gray scale of self-discovery. Who didn't answer questions with "Well, that's what the Bible says." Who knew that a good person could disagree with other good people. Who didn't fear their own mind. Who saw the big picture and said, "Isn't it messy and beautiful?"

Of course, if I knew what to look for, I would have realized those people had been around me all along. But I needed someone who looked like me, talked like me, translated the world in a way I understood. That's the fresh commission on every human life. There is no one exactly like you. And yet there are many who are similar to you, and have never felt seen or understood. You never know who is watching and who needs you to express it all.

How's that for some cheese?

THE VIEW FROM my chair in the living room. The crappy little table I bought online. My two-dollar succulents. My hummingbird feeder. I stare at them like I would a sleeping lover, heartwarmed that they are unaware of their beauty.

How miraculous to be conscious. To be the result of random molecules, procreating for billions of years, waking up into selfhood and belief. Sometimes I feel like we don't belong here, like we screw everything up on this planet as if we're an invasive species. But this planet made us. Or perhaps some kind of god or overmind made us, to bring it pleasure or company.

It's just all such a marvel. I am a conscious bag of atoms, many of which were in the bodies of dinosaurs, and now they bounce around in me. I was either created with meaning, or I wasn't, and find meaning everywhere anyway. Imagine if humans are just random molecules, and yet we write novels. We, meaningless matter, write stories about fictional meaningless matter, to make ourselves feel things, even sadness.

Why am I astonished? This is the one and only world any of us know. Why should we find it strange? And yet we do.

A PARABLE: A thousand years ago, God appeared to a boy in the desert and gave him a piece of glass. God said, "You can hold this glass in your hand and see the whole world. Whatever you want to know, it is in there."

The boy said, "But how? This piece of glass is so small. How can I know the world?"

God said, "You will know it like drops of water. One drop at a time. You will collect puddles of the world, and you will think you know it. But you will not. You cannot know the wholeness of the ocean by looking at its drops. You will fight your brother because his drops are different than yours. You will imagine different wholes. You will blame the tide on the tide pools. You will believe driftwood is bones."

The boy replied, "But I want to know as much as I can."

God said, "I know, son. You will love the glass. And you will stare into it with love in your mind. You will stop seeing and smelling the bigness of the world around your body. You will be drunk with obsession for tiny keyholes into every other place but your own."

The boy said, "Then why would you give me this? Why would I want bits of information if you tell me they will betray the real whole?"

God said, "You cannot possibly understand now. Did

Judas understand his role in the story of everything? The world is healed by mistakes."

OFTEN, WHEN I am trying to write about my life, my experience feels so unique that it cannot be spoken about with clarity, it can only be felt. But when I talk about it, almost every time, I find friends leaning in and saying, "Me, too." My Christian friends say, "Me, too." My Jewish and Muslim friends say, "Me, too." My faithless friends say, "Tell me more."

The music we make can be transposed into many keys. Tradition versus expression. Family and freedom. To stay or to go. To love your captors. To hurt the ones you love by prioritizing survival over comfort. To change so drastically that your prior self feels like a completely different person.

I miss church. The songs and seeing friends and lunch after service, sitting outside on a Sunday afternoon. I travel too much these days to have a dependable routine, so I rarely get to go. But when the mysterious world hides its beauty from me, and I feel only chaos and hurt, I miss the old certainty I had among the pews. Of worrying about which Christian CD was okay to listen to, which book was "biblical" enough, which candidate was pro-life enough to get my vote. I miss walking down the street, knowing I was eternal and my soul was safe. Nowhere seeing the disconnect between my comfort in the love of Jesus and the thought of billions burning for eternity all around me. If I'd ever really believed it, I think I'd have been weeping and gnashing my teeth in the streets to save just one more soul.

But I liked being told what to believe. I think most people do. It's hard to think for yourself. So much responsibility. I liked getting caught up in the momentum of a pastor who believed in his words. There was a thrill to feeling God's watchful and angry eye. Now I feel God's all-embracing patience, which feels cosmically true, but less safe. An angry father is at least paying attention, caring what I do. A distant sage allows me to stumble, and then asks me to learn.

WHILE WALKING THROUGH the woods as a kid, I would bust and push my way through thickets and cut my arms and squint my eyes. And then I would find a deer trail. A path well worn by generations of deer. Over time, they walked and found the best way through. And by using it often, they kept it smooth and free from overgrowth. The deer had no survey men, no instruments or contractors. All they had were the deer before them.

I spent my twenties preaching, the classic folly of the young. I'm calmer now, more confident that the truth of the universe is fearless and kind, patient and hidden in plain sight. And now that I'm through the thicket, I'm finding a well-worn path. Full of ten-point bucks and regal does with quiet steps.

DRIVING ALONG THE beach in Big Sur, I couldn't see fifteen feet in front of me. The fog was a blindfold, cold and gray-white, covering the Pacific Coast Highway and the places where the mountains hit the sea. But I turned off the road, away from the ocean, and went up the steep switchbacks. I climbed up and found that the blindness went only so high.

Above the fog, it was as clear as a desert sky. And there she was, the sun, still shining. The fog that had covered me looked different from above. What was blinding then now showed itself as an endless rolling blanket, soft and shiny in the sun.

It's nice to imagine how God would see all this muck and confusion of human society. It calms me down.

IMAGINE BEING A baby in your mother's womb, and having consciousness. You have arms and legs and lungs and eyes and a mouth, but are completely flabbergasted as to why. All you've ever done is float in that warm juice. You think your body's features are useless. A waste.

Life is comfortable and cozy in your cocoon. You can't imagine anything better than your current life. And you have no idea that it will ever change. But your strange body, equipped with so many useless tools, nags you. You flip and kick, testing them out. And you make a million guesses, probably all wrong. Then one day, your whole life changes. A scary transition happens. You're moved into a strange world where you feel helpless and terrible. Now the body you had all along becomes profoundly useful. Your lungs fill with this mysterious thing called air.

This analogy was given to me by a pastor years ago. Even if we don't know what's coming, the analogy says, we were made for it. He was talking about heaven, but I think the description works for more than that. I think it works for life. I know so many people who went through confusing labyrinths before arriving at contentment and joy and a career they love. In their twenties or thirties, they worked random jobs where they felt useless and wondered what it all meant. They couldn't have known that working this odd job or that would be the thing that gave them the idea to start their own thing. Going to that random city was how they met their wife. They didn't know that the angst of discontent was prepping them for destiny.

Sometimes I think we're still in the womb, kicking at the walls, feeling too big for our cocoon, and thinking nothing will ever change.

Acknowledgments

Thank you, Derek Reed, for making the process of writing a book fun, and therapeutic, and encouraging. For being the editor and therefore perfecter of dreams. I can't believe any good books exist without your touch. Thank you, Ashley Hong, for spotting the things I'd never see, for being integral and necessary and kind. Thank you, Bryan Norman, for being my advocate and honest friend, and basically part of my family. Thank you, Tina Constable, for going on that morning swim and naming this book, and for continuing to coax me out of imposter syndrome.

ABOUT THE AUTHOR

JEDIDIAH JENKINS is a travel writer, an entrepreneur, and the *New York Times* bestselling author of *To Shake the Sleeping Self*. A graduate of USC and Pepperdine University School of Law, Jenkins began his professional career with the nonprofit Invisible Children, where he helped orchestrate multinational campaigns to end the use of child soldiers in central Africa. His parents, Peter and Barbara Jenkins, are the authors of the bestselling A Walk Across America series. He is the executive editor of *Wilderness* magazine. Jenkins's work has appeared in *The Paris Review* and *Playboy*, and he has been covered by *National Geographic*.

jedidiahjenkins.com
Facebook: @jedidiahjenkinswriter
Twitter: @jedidiahjenkins
Instagram: @jedidiahjenkins

ABOUT THE TYPE

This book was set in Sabon, a typeface designed by the well-known German typographer Jan Tschichold (1902–74). Sabon's design is based upon the original letter forms of sixteenth-century French type designer Claude Garamond and was created specifically to be used for three sources: foundry type for hand composition, Linotype, and Monotype. Tschichold named his typeface for the famous Frankfurt typefounder Jacques Sabon (c. 1520–80).